JACOB MUNDT

# PROFOUND LIGHT

## *Overcoming Childhood and Adolescent Trauma*

outskirts
press

NOTE: The author decided to keep all last names out of this book to protect specific individuals' identities and privacy, except for one name and the foreword section. Due to certain circumstances, the author had to change some characters' names altogether additionally.

With certain privacy matters, the author also decided to keep some real locations and full names of places/businesses out of this book.

## Dedication

*The author dedicates this book to the loving memory of his Aunt Sue, his Grandma Mary, and his Grandpa Loren. Your family and friends both love and miss you.*

*For anyone suffering from any despair, know that you are never alone, and through light, you find hope and closure and the purpose in your life to keep moving forward.*

-Jacob Mundy

# Table of Contents

# Preface

Whenever I talk to my grandpa on my dad's side of the family on the phone, I always enjoy hearing the touching words, "I'm proud of you, Jacob." My grandpa has not been the only one to tell me this, as many of my beloved family members and friends have reiterated those words to me many times. They all have not said those words just because of my life's accomplishments, but how I have overcome the severe trauma I endured in my young and adolescent years. They say it because I now stand tall. Even today, I still can recall a few times when a friend of one of my family members learned of my story and expressed similar empathy. After so long, I started asking myself, how can I pass what symbol of hope I have become through my story to others who need a reason to keep pushing on in this challenging life and world?

At the same time, I also wanted to find a way to grow as a cancer and mental health advocate. I wanted to share my story with people outside of my family and friends. When I brainstormed ideas to accomplish both thoughts, it was only a few months after my college graduation and receiving my bachelor's degree. At first, my mind was blank, so I decided not to overthink it. Instead, I put some thought into it when I was not working at my first out-of-college job. Towards the end of 2021, an idea came to mind.

What if I shoot for the stars and write a memoir about the trauma that I faced throughout the childhood and adolescent years of my life? I would admit, even to myself, that it sounded wild, mainly because I had never worked on a book. However, after carefully thinking about how powerful my story could be to others and the opportunities that could come with working on a book project, and with my passion for storytelling, it sounded like a much better idea.

Before I knew it, I started working on the book development. By January 2022, I had an outline completed. I wrote down enough information on my vision for this project and the outline itself. It took me around eleven months to write the first draft, and I finished it in June 2023. I knew there was no turning back after completing it. I needed to see the entire project entirely through, no matter how extremely painful reverting to those dark memories in my childhood and adolescent years was, and the rest is history.

# Foreword (John T.)

June 1999 marked the beginning of a journey, which would forever intertwine the lives of me and Jacob. During this time, the stage was set for a remarkable story of resilience, growth, and the power of human connection. It was during this time that I joined the Illinois Army National Guard. Here I met Jacob's father.

As our paths converged, I became aware of the challenges Jacob encountered in his early years. Born the previous year, Jacob faced numerous health obstacles. His young life had been marked by adversity. Over the course of the next six years, Jacob's father and I served side by side, forming a bond forged by shared experiences and a deep sense of camaraderie. Our journey together reached its pinnacle when we embarked on an arduous eighteen-month deployment to Iraq, where we faced the realities and hardships of war together.

In the following years, life took its course. I found myself separated from Jacob's story, receiving only sporadic updates through his father. However, in 2018 as I embarked on a new endeavor, the launch of the Levitt AMP Music Series, our paths were destined to cross again. Amid organizing this series, we found ourselves in need of additional support. I recalled hearing that Jacob harbored an interest in broadcasting. Seeing the opportunity, I reached out to Jacob, asking if he would be willing to volunteer his time to assist with stage setup and teardown during the concerts.

With unwavering enthusiasm, Jacob eagerly accepted the invitation. During this time, I witnessed the remarkable transformation he had undergone. Now a young man on the cusp of his college years, Jacob displayed a level of maturity, dedication, and resilience that left an indelible impression on me. His commitment and tireless efforts over the course of that year and the next were nothing but extraordinary. As I watched him grow and evolve, I could not help but marvel at the immense strides he had taken.

Jacob's journey did not end with his college graduation. As a testament to the meaningful connections, a relationship he had forged during his volunteer work at the concerts had blossomed into a job opportunity. Jacob became employed as an editor and photojournalist at a local television station, a feat that would be a significant accomplishment for anyone. Yet, considering the trials and tribulations he had overcome, it was nothing short of a miraculous achievement.

Examining Jacob's life, one cannot help but recognize the presence of countless miracles that have shaped his path. Still, I am convinced that these miracles were not mere happenstance. Instead, these demonstrated Jacob's unwavering spirit and his determination to make the most of his life. His unyielding work ethic, kindness, optimism, and capacity for forgiveness have not only touched my own life but are virtues from which we can all learn and grow.

As I pen these words, I hope the story of Jacob Mundy

will serve as a source of inspiration and a reminder. We possess the strength to overcome and flourish even in the face of adversity. Jacob's journey serves as a powerful testament to the resilience of the human spirit and the transformative power of compassion and perseverance.

May the pages that follow illuminate the remarkable life of Jacob Mundy; a life shaped by miracles. May his story inspire us all to embrace the qualities that define his remarkable character.

# Prologue

I could feel a funnel of emotions go through my body as my mother and me got off the United Airlines plane at the Memphis International Airport. I was arriving for my yearly checkup for my childhood cancer battle at St. Jude Children's Research Hospital. Almost every emotion from happiness, excitement, nervousness, and more filled my airway as we walked to the baggie claim area to meet with a St. Jude shuttle bus driver. They would take us to a hotel close to the St. Jude Hospital. This June 2019 visit would be different than my previous checkups, as it would be my final year of regular doctor visits. After this year, I would return to Memphis solely every five years for my St. Jude life study checkups through the St. Jude life study program; a program to study the late effects of treatment while still ensuring the survivor participants that no signs of cancer were found.

I could not be prouder of myself, for I had hopefully reaching the ten-year remission mark of not having Non-Hodgkin's Lymphoma mark that year. What I had overcame throughout my life and how I reached my own profound triumph was another unique story in an enormous amount of miracle stories around the world. All were not just related to the St. Jude Hospital. I was happy and excited to return to the place I have always considered a second home since the conclusion of my cancer battles. More importantly, I could not be more excited to once again see the St. Jude Hospital that impacted my life through my childhood cancer battles while seeing some of the staff members that helped me beat cancer. I could not deny though how nervous I became before my first day of appointments over one question. The question being, would I reach the top and be able to go home with the news that no signs of cancerous tumors were found during my checkup?

I had faced so much misfortune, adversity, and uncertainty throughout my childhood and adolescent years. So, I could not help but wonder about that question. My mother has always told me, "Life is a rollercoaster; you will have your ups and downs." I cannot deny my mother is not wrong on what she meant through the statement. Still, I wanted my happy ending, and I wanted to find the remaining peace I had found through healing from my trauma. During my childhood and adolescent years, I faced the unbelievable with my two cancer battles. I had endured so many more traumatic battles but fought with every instinct in my body to overcome those barriers.

A few days went by, and it was time for my last appointment before my mother and I headed back home; my dad, who had driven down to be there for me, also headed back home. The last appointment would be simple, as it was basically a regular meeting between us and my life study team to go over the results of the testing. The testing came back all clear, and I was officially a person that was in remission from a life-threatening disease for ten years. The hope, self-resilience, and many other themes I carried with me throughout my traumatic battles of my youth and adolescent years had remained with me.

From that day on, I knew that my journey of healing from the trauma I endured was complete. The Jacob who had gone down a road of destruction through the turmoil of his trauma many years ago was a memory of the past. I gave into the darkness years ago when I found myself breaking down mentally after years of physical and mental battles. I had turned to worse ways to cope with the emotional pain. The weight of enduring the trauma after so long turned into a battle for control over my thoughts and an ultimate struggle to lift me back up from the ground. Nevertheless, now being a cancer survivor and ten years in remission, I reached the top of the mountain and crafted my own extraordinary destiny. I accomplished the nearly impossible tasks of having finished the journey of healing from the trauma I went through all those years.

# 1

# Setting the Stage

Like many, I only remember a small portion of my childhood. However, I still do remember the early part of it. I was born on July 27th, 1998, at the Cottage Hospital in Galesburg, Illinois. My parents, my two older half-sisters, and I lived in a three-bedroom house for most of my early childhood. The house we were in at the time was not the biggest, but it still managed to fit all of us. My older half-brother lived with his mother in a different area. Despite this, my father did whatever he could to ensure we spent as much time together as possible.

My mother took a job as a certified nursing assistant (CNA) at 19, only switching to a few separate locations over the years. Her first CNA job was at the Marigold nursing home in Galesburg, Illinois, where she met my father, a fellow CNA. Even before they met, my father served with the National Guard part-time a few times a week in addition to his regular CNA job. He wanted to make a difference in his life and exhibited an attitude of giving back to people in despair. He just needed people to know someone was there to lend a helping hand. One of the major benefits of my dad serving in the

National Guard was the many lasting friendships he developed with many of his fellow soldiers.

My father has always enjoyed doing woodcraft projects. He would often put them together from scratch, such as little selves, and so on, which became one of our favorite father-son bonding activities. He would bring many creative ideas with the tools he had available to use. Some projects were small, and others were bigger and more challenging, but we still overcame that obstacle every time. The unique part is that he always stayed connected with that creative habit.

For the entirety of my childhood and up until after receiving my bachelor's degree, I grew up as a "town boy," living in a small town about twenty miles from my birthplace. The town we resided in had only a few businesses and no grocery stores. For us, though, the quiet vibe in the town was an upside compared to what it could not offer. One of my family members who lived in the town was the owner of a successful food business. Her restaurant became a popular place for my family and other residents living in the town to eat at. One of the ways to kill time was to go to the town's small bowling alley, which became a popular activity for me and my family. For movie nights, we went to the locally owned movie rental store in town because digital streaming services were not available back then.

Upon my birth into this world, my parents could not ignore one problem they had noticed. Usually, newborns' heads are a standard circle type; but my head turned out to be oval. My mother's obstetrician assumed this was caused by the problematic childbirth my mother experienced. The doctor recommended we see my pediatrician if they saw no change. By the time I was nine months old, nothing changed, and my head shape remained unnatural.

My parents could not get over the thought that it was

something more. My mother took me back to my pediatrician. He did not know what to say to ease my parents' feelings, and the only thought he could think of was additional testing. My pediatrician then decided to have a computed axial tomography (CAT) scan scheduled. While he did not have an answer, my pediatrician agreed to refer me to a learning program nearby for children zero to three years old named "Abilities Plus." The program was for children like me struggling to reach the milestones children were naturally supposed to be reaching at my age.

After waiting about four months for me to have a CAT scan done, my parents took me to the Cottage Hospital (the same hospital where I was born). My parents found out the scan had shown moderate dubitation on the ventricular system. The pediatrician diagnosed me with Macrocephaly with Ventriculomegaly, and developmental delays. For anyone who does not know what it could mean, here is a little explanation of each word. Macrocephaly is a term used to describe when an infant's head circumference is more extensive than what a normal infant's head is supposed to be. Ventriculomegaly is when the ventricles (particles in a brain) appear larger than they should.

Even with the answer, my parents had a tough time believing life plagued me with the unwanted diagnosis at such an early age. While my pediatrician was sure his conclusion could not be inaccurate, he wanted to send us to the Children's Hospital of Iowa (aka Iowa City) for more testing and to see a neurologist who could give my parents a confirmed answer. After analyzing the prior CAT scan and more physical examinations, the neurologist there confirmed the diagnosis of 'Macrocephaly with Ventriculomegaly.' At the time, the neurologist decided that I did not need a shunt for the extra fluid in my head, which is a typical treatment for children with my diagnosis. While there was the side of my parents that was happy it was not a life-threatening diagnosis, the other side of them was heartbroken. At the same time as that occurrence, another threat came into my life. Unlike healthy nine-month-olds, I was not crawling or moving around. I was also not showing any signs of trying to communicate via speaking. As concerned as they should have been, my parents mentioned this to my pediatrician. Meanwhile, I did further tests to find the truth behind my odd head growth. My pediatrician decided to have doctors at the Children's Hospital of Iowa look further into the situation while I kept undergoing tests for my odd head shape. While the doctors at the Children's Hospital of Iowa did not think there were any false findings in the previous analysis, they still wanted to review and re-analyze the previous tests.

Sadly, the doctor's words shed no light. He fully confirmed I had a developmental delay. Since my father received special education in early grade school for several months, the doctors tied my diagnosis to genetic hierarchy. Later testing showed that despite the diagnosis having no impact on my general health, the diagnosis would still impact my communication and motor movements. There was no better approach to getting where I needed to be than continuing the early intervention program through "Abilities Plus." Although, I showed continued progress, I would still have to remain in occupational, speech, and physical therapy to continue developing those domains further. I did start walking at fourteen months, but I still failed to show any signs of language via speaking.

While I was too young to comprehend the misfortune fully, it was painful. I would admit I know, as well as others, that life comes with at least one or two bumps as you grow up. For me, though, to experience two primary life-changing diagnoses that early on was just a lot to handle for my parents and me. Yes, even though both diagnoses were not life-threatening, they had a significant impact on me. Both would later keep on darkly plaguing my life.

Looking back on those events, I am bittersweet. Still, I still see the hidden light in the situation that I do today. Both diagnoses still allowed me to continue living life without worrying about either one attempting to end my life. Life gave me two awful conditions that no child should have to endure, but they did not define me going forward. Either I could have been angry at God, or I could have moved on. I could have continued learning how to effectively live life with both conditions.

# 2

# Painful Discovery

Around my third birthday, I started experiencing on-and-off days of fevers and stomach aches. My worried parents took me to my regular pediatrician. He thought it was just a common viral infection and prescribed an antibiotic to help take care of it. With all the common colds and infections going on at the time, my parents thought it was not serious. And so, they put the thought of it being a more significant condition behind them.

After several days, my mother noticed the right side of my groin area was swollen when she changed my diaper. Because my parents noticed my left side was normal, both of them started getting worried again. The following morning, they immediately called my pediatrician to have me seen. Though to our disappointment, he did not know what could be wrong. He then referred me to a Cottage Hospital surgeon for a truthful answer.

He, too, was unsure what was going on but ordered a CAT scan immediately. He informed my parents that the scan showed a mass, which he had thought was a growth of a cyst.

Without any hesitation, he scheduled me for surgery that very day. Numerous family members from both my mom's and dad's sides made the trip to the hospital to sit in the waiting room with my parents. The surgery was initially supposed to take an hour but took much longer than my family had expected. Several hours later, the doctor came out and gave the outcome of the surgery. My family did not want to believe the horror that came out of the doctor's mouth as he finally walked into the waiting room, giving them an answer to what was going on.

Even my mom could see the horror in his eyes as he informed my family I had cancer. And it was malignant. Every single family member in the room was devastated by my awful diagnosis. More importantly, they were so confused about why this had to happen to me and what exactly I did to deserve the diagnosis. All we could think about was if it were my time to go up in the sky, but I was just too young to go up to heaven.

I was in surgery for what seemed like the longest time; and, for my family, an eternity. By the end of the surgery, doctors removed my appendix, a part of my colon, and a tumor the size of a tennis ball. By a good miracle, the doctor removed most of the cancer. But sadly, doctors could not remove five percent of the tumor. After the surgery was over, a nurse took me back to the recovery room, where my parents and sisters waited to see what the next steps were. The following morning, an ambulance transferred me to Saint Francis Hospital in Peoria. As soon as I arrived there, doctors felt I needed to go to the pediatrics unit, so a cancer specialist from the St. Jude Children's Research Hospital Peoria-affiliated clinic could further help me.

She could not point out exactly what type of cancer I had. With the various kinds of cancer, she could not start discussing treatment options until the results of the biopsy from the tumor came back and it showed what type of cancer lurked inside my body. Until then, I remained in the hospital to recover from the surgery. Both family and friends stopped by to see how I was doing. All brought gifts to help lift our spirits broken by the cancer diagnosis. To my surprise, despite still feeling sore, I woke up to go to the play area on the pediatrics floor.

What seemed like forever, but was only a couple of days, passed before the specialist walked into the room to reveal the results from the biopsy. The results returned with a positive indication of non-Hodgkin's Burkitt's Lymphoma. My family became confused about how I still ended up with such a horrible disease, along with all the medical parts associated with the actual cancer treatment. My entire family undoubtedly felt all kinds of destructive emotions while standing in front of a child with a severe disease.

Along with the horrible news, the specialist had mentioned only one treatment option to kill the remaining portion of the tumor. While radiation was one effective cancer treatment option, the best option was chemotherapy, but with treatment came an unexpected circumstance. The specialist explained that the Peoria-affiliated clinic did not have all the resources to treat my cancer, including the proper medical equipment. Therefore, I needed to go to the main St. Jude Children's Research Hospital in Memphis, Tennessee. However, there was a slight chance I could finish the treatment at the Peoria-affiliated clinic, but my cancer was already at stage three and rapidly growing. So, I would have to start the treatment immediately once we arrived in Memphis.

Saying goodbye to the family for at least the duration of the cancer treatment was extremely hard, especially for my mom and dad. We spent as much time with family and friends as possible before getting on the flight to Memphis. All my family and friends expressed an incredible amount of love and concern. My mom even had to go home that night to pack and figure out which family member my sisters would stay with while we were gone. The very next day, my sisters came to the hospital to be with us that entire day.

However, because of the fussy brat I was due to the soreness and pain I felt, I refused anyone (and yes, even my family) to touch or hold me. Everyone at the time was from both sides of the family. All the temporary goodbyes were a lot for my parents and me. What was even worse was the level of uncertainty about if I would come back alive. Despite St. Jude having exceptional childhood cancer survival rates, cancer was still a life-threatening disease. It still left everyone feeling uncertain.

The time came for the final goodbyes, but all the family knew God was there with us to help guide us along the way. A nurse removed my intravenous (IV) drip the following day before my discharge from St Francis. The three-hour flight to Memphis, with a layover in Detroit, was unbearable. Even I could not lie that all that went through my parents' and my mind was the chance of me not coming back alive.

Later that morning, we finally arrived at the St. Jude Children's Research Hospital in Memphis. My parents could not believe what the hospital looked like in person. At that point, we hoped we finally found a bright light and a cure for the dark-growing disease. Because I was so young, losing me to cancer would be just too much for my friends and family.

# 3

# First Round

Upon my arrival to the hospital, I was immediately taken to the admitting area, where my parents filled out the first sets of paperwork before I could receive any care. Once my parents completed the necessary paperwork, a hospital worker showed us the new area called "assessment and triage." By this point, my parents just wanted the whole ordeal to be behind us. Unfortunately, I had to go through the initial start of a typical doctor's checkup.

The cycle included a nurse taking my vitals and checking my weight and doing blood work to check my current levels. Despite feeling like it took years, the nurse only took about an hour to do everything. While it may have felt like a routine checkup, we all knew it was about to be life and death for me. One of the truths about cancer is that no matter how happy you are, a cancer diagnosis can easily take away all the happiness and joy in a matter of seconds.

The unique part about the St. Jude Hospital in Memphis are the different clinics it offers to deliver the best treatment and support for every family who walks through the door, no matter the cancer type or circumstance. A clinic was my spot for the many update meetings throughout my treatment. B Clinic housed the Stem Cell/Bone Marrow Transplant unit, C Clinic housed specialty cancers, D Clinic housed Solid Tumors, E Clinic housed the Neuro-Oncology/Brain Tumors, and H Clinic housed Hematology. The hospital has several other clinics to provide the best patient services, including the Surgery Clinic, Cardiopulmonary Services, Dental Clinic, Diagnostic Imaging, Medicine Room, Procedural Recovery Area, Child Life, Patient Pharmacy, Psychosocial Services, School Programs, and many others.

The Medicine Room was familiar since it allowed out-patients to quickly receive needed medicine without going through the "entire normal admitting hospital process." St. Jude wanted patients to have as much time in an environment outside of the hospital setting as possible. They knew, as many incoming families do, that every sick child deserves to try to enjoy life while receiving treatment, especially since every family deserves to spend time with their child in a normal environmental setting.

Before I could go up to a hospital room, I went into one of the rooms in A Clinic, where two doctors walked in to talk about my situation. One of the least fun parts of going through such treatment is a procedure to get a central line put into your chest. While that word might seem scary to an average person, for cancer patients, a central line makes treatment a lot easier. Instead of a nurse poking my skin with a needle to inject my chemo or any medicine, they would have easy access through a central line.

The downside to the central line was the handful of oral medicine I would still have to take by mouth. To prevent infection or problems with the central line, one of the nurses gave my parents a crash course on taking care of a central line. Therefore, it would remain in shape when I was not in the hospital receiving the treatments. Even though I would now be walking around with a good-sized bump on my chest, not having to suffer through the pain of a needle was a clever idea. Plus, there were several times I got a funny facial reaction from a stranger thinking, "Why does that kid have a bump on his chest?" which was always worth it.

Neither doctor wasted any time discussing a detailed treatment plan with an extremely high chance of survival. Even with the significant amount of the tumor removed during surgery, the remaining portion of the tumor was still enough to kill me if left untreated. The doctors did fully confirm that my cancer type was non-Hodgkin's Lymphoma. To get rid of the remaining portion of the tumor, I would need a high chemotherapy dose. Unfortunately, because the Peoria clinic did not yet have the treatment resources, we would have to remain in Memphis for my full five months of chemotherapy.

The survival rate at the Memphis St. Jude Hospital for overall childhood cancer was more than eighty percent. However, because I was at stage three at the time of my diagnosis, I would have to endure aggressive therapy. While my parents knew what to do, it would still be hard for my mom to be far away from my sisters. One of my beloved close family members was more than willing to let my sisters stay over at her house. They would watch them through the duration of my treatment.

When I was not in the hospital receiving treatment, we would stay in a building called "The Ronald McDonald House." The Ronald McDonald House is unlike anything anybody could dream of, and even still, what it sounds like does not do it full justice. It was not just a place for a patient to stay but a house built on love and hope. For patients, it was a well-needed message that they were not the only ones fighting the ugly disease. Moreover, it gave families the hope they desperately needed. Families were supported by staff and each other because of the commonality with the other families.

The building was like a hotel and is one of the handful of places outside the St. Jude Hospital campus for families to stay during their child's treatment. A significant part of the place is the family atmosphere that exists there. Most of the families staying there also had a loved one diagnosed with cancer. Despite the unfortunate nightmare of having a loved one with cancer, staying at the Ronald McDonald House provided the comfort my family needed. When the doctors told us of my cancer, it caused so much agony; though being in that "family-like environment" made us feel like we were not alone and, more importantly, that my family was not the only one going through an unimaginable nightmare.

Each room had two full-sized beds, two dressers, one closet, a bathroom, and a few other amenities that would typically be in a hotel room. Everyone shared the kitchens and dining rooms on the main floor. The extras and amenities were there to give the families the best experience possible. The back patio is one of the most popular areas, as most families spend a lot of time there. The area included a basketball hoop, a large open concrete section for the patients to run around in, some tables and chairs for the families to relax and talk, and a toy car I would get in every chance I could.

Just as the hospital staff was essential to the families, the Ronald McDonald House staff was equally important. The staff would always treat patients as if they were their children. They wanted to show how much they cared and helped take the patients' minds off the reality they were facing. One massive way the staff showed their support was through the many general and annual holiday events. These ensured patients and families would always have an enormous amount of comfort from the staff themselves. I would be lying if I said I did not find kid ways to torment some staff, including "the shuttle bus driver," but it was just a way to show them I knew they cared so much for all the patients.

As it was at the hospital, various groups often came to the Ronald McDonald House and showed their support whenever possible. One occasion was a youth group from a local church. Another was a couple of people from the Southern Cruisers Riding Motorcycle Club (who even gave me a ride!). As much as the patients looked forward to those events, they looked forward to more of the activities put on every holiday. One of my favorites was Halloween: a day filled with pumpkin decorating, craft decorating, costume dressing, and trick-or-treating inside the building.

Before we knew it, I officially started my first chemo treatment. For almost five months, I would have to endure six high-dose courses of chemo injected through my central line, along with other various IV medications to help with the immediate side effects of the rough chemo. During each course, I would stay in a room at the hospital on the second floor for five to seven days. After I had finished the current chemo dose, I would go back to the Ronald McDonald House to recoup, recover, and let my body build up what strength it could for the next round of chemo.

On the outside, the chemotherapy seemed like it was barely doing anything, but it hit the inside of my body like a professional National Football League (NFL) player had run into me and knocked me to the ground. The most challenging aspect with the doses of the chemotherapy was how I would only get to spend a few days at a time at Ronald McDonald House before I returned to the hospital with low blood counts. Once my count level rose above five hundred, I would return to Ronald McDonald House. At that point, it was tremendously hard to tell if the chemo was killing off the tumor cells or if it was killing the other essential body cells.

Further news from the doctors revealed that a couple of tests showed that the cancer had not spread anymore. Still, it left us further wondering if a light was going to arrive at the end of the journey. There were times when the pain was at a minimum and I was in the mood to get up and move around. Then, there were times when I was not feeling up to it. It was not that I did not want to get up and move around and not be in bed all day, every day. I did not feel up to it, given the circumstances at the time. So, my parents had to do whatever they could to motivate me to get up and move around when the pain levels were low. I mean, when you were a kid, you had so much energy; however, I just felt like the chemotherapy was taking up all the energy inside of me. In the end, though, I had to do whatever to keep pushing forward.

Even with my decrease of energy on the inside due to a combo of the pain from the remaining portion of the tumor and the physical impact of the treatment, the adventurous kid partly remained the same inside. I somehow managed to find the courage to get up out of my hospital bed and sit by my parents or when a nurse would come in to check up on me and even hold me. I loved all my nurses equally. I would admit, though, that there was one I let hold me more often than the other nurses, and I never gave her any problems.

Sometimes, I just got up and moved around in my room. Many times, I got up to move outside my hospital room. I went to the play area a few floors below to the small entertainment room near the nurse's station or even for a quick wagon ride, which quickly became one of my activities. The advantage of the treatment was that no matter which hospital room St. Jude assigned a patient to, an IV pole with wheels was in every room. So, a patient could either walk around in the room or go outside of the room and move around.

As much as I wanted to be lazy and remain sitting in the hospital bed, it was not an option. To keep my strength and functions going strong, I would often go through rehab and go through both physical and occupational therapy. St. Jude has many hospital areas for different resources, so there was a separate area for the rehab services. It is a service for current and former cancer patients returning for a checkup, with all the current adaptations in technology. It was not my favorite activity, but I had to do rehab to make sure my body stayed in decent shape. I had to also keep it as strong as possible to help the chemo fight my cancer.

For some reason, even today, I cannot wrap my head around how sometimes I thought the couch in my hospital room felt more comfortable to nap on instead of my hospital bed. Most of the time, especially during the night, I passed out on my hospital bed, but there were times when I decided to take a nap on the couch. The treatment, of course, not only made some of my body weak but also made me exhausted. It caused me to sleep a lot during the day. At least I can say all the sleeping allowed me to completely forget I was a helpless, sick cancer patient and forget about my current horrible reality.

Despite my family doing their best to hide their emotions, at that age, a part of me knew deep inside the feelings of emptiness and hopelessness that filled the room. Who could blame any of them for what they had to see with their own eyes? Whether we liked it or not, I was a child with a disease that could put me closer to being underground at any second; an actual reality and a living nightmare for my family and friends. As much as the treatment was complex for me, it was harder for my family to see me suffer like that and be able to truly do little to help me.

However, what comforted us was all the families at the hospital and Ronald McDonald House going through the same ordeal. It was so easy for my family, especially both of my parents, to lock themselves away from the world because of having to see their own loved one go through a horrible circumstance. Being around other families going through the same ordeal gave them so much hope that, no matter what lay ahead, they would not be alone. There would always be someone to talk to. They understood what my family was going through, and my family understood what the other families were going through as well. When you have someone going through a comparable situation, there is a feeling of comfort and knowing the exact sorrow associated with it.

Since we could not go back home until I had finished treatment, many of my family members would come to Memphis to visit. It did not matter if they came to the hospital with us, the Ronald McDonald House, or if we went somewhere in Memphis near the St. Jude Hospital campus. We found something to do. One unforgettable memory was when one of my grandpas came and brought both of my sisters with him, which also marked the end of another round of chemo. It is so weird because the chemo made time freeze, but it went by so fast at the same time. All three of them ended up staying for an entire week. We ended up not doing many activities outside of the hospital's campus and decided to do stuff in the back play area of the building. All of them were by our side once again, and that is all that mattered.

Not long after their departure back home, one of my aunts

and uncles came down for a visit. Since I did not feel too bad or was not in significant pain, we all took a trip to Memphis Zoo. Seeing all the different animals and experiencing life outside of treatment was so cool. The best part of my aunt and uncle coming down was the unique gift they got me.

On one of the sides of the Ronald McDonald House is a section of lines of small in-ground bricks. Anyone could buy a brick for someone of their choosing, but most of the bricks were either for a cancer patient who stayed there during their treatment or someone whose life had ended by cancer. While down in Memphis, my beloved aunt and uncle honored my journey by buying me a brick. As much as that gesture brought comfort to me, it was also a comfort for my parents and a great reminder that my whole family was still thinking of me, even with being many miles away.

The most remarkable memory at Ronald McDonald House was the day I made my mark on the handprint wall. There were two areas of walls inside the building that were blank canvases, so the building owners let the patients currently residing there have the option of leaving their own stories there. Using actual hand paint, every patient could pick a color and dip the palm of their hands into the paint and onto the wall, along with the name, age, cancer type, and hometown location. It will always be special because I knew my story would live on, even if I made it to remission.

The nurses and doctors (but, really the entire staff at St. Jude) were the real heroes who kept the spirits up in all the St. Jude families. It was not just because it is their job to provide care for the patients, but because they genuinely care for every patient and their families. The nurses and doctors do not go into the medical field to help sick or injured people. Instead, they do it because they believe in a higher purpose than themselves. For all of them, it was not just a job; it was them all wanting to make a significant difference in the lives of both the cancer patients and their families.

Most importantly, they give so much hope to every family that walks through the door and the believable truth that they were not alone in the fight. To them, losing a patient would be like losing their own child. Every staff member at St. Jude treats the children as if they were their children, and that is what makes the hospital one of the best hospitals there is. Every patient there walked out with a special meaning and hope from the experience St. Jude gave them after moving on to become a cancer survivor.

# 4

# False Hope

My parents and I will never forget the day we finally got some amazing news. A small group of nurses entered the room with balloons, a T-shirt, and a necklace. For the first time, my tests came back all clear without any signs of cancerous tumors in my body. I had finally beaten potential death firsthand, and my medical team officially declared me in remission.

Everyone around me and back home got the bright light we all deserved and hoped for before walking through the doors of St. Jude. Both my mother's and father's eyes were filled with joy and happiness that everything would be okay. My parents got their beloved son back, and I got a chance to return to being a normal kid. Hopefully, I could experience growing up without any more adversity. I had overcome an intense obstacle that no child should have to endure, but it made me a stronger person at the end of the battle.

After I battled the disease for a little over four and a half months, St. Jude gave us the full clearance to go back home shortly before Christmas of 2001. My return home brought massive joy and endless happiness to all my family members and friends. Numerous family members and friends came over to visit and celebrate, including family members who had not seen us since we left for Memphis. As wonderful as it was just to be back home, it was more wonderful to be back together with my entire family. Not even my bald head ruined the blessing. I was finally back where I belonged and united with my loved ones.

While my parents and I were beyond grateful we were finally back home with my beloved family, the miraculous experience St. Jude gave us forever remained with us. The work at St. Jude was a straight example of God's grace and the unbelievable miracles of God's angels. We saw firsthand what miracles could happen when people come together. The St. Jude staff chooses the career they do because they all believe in a higher purpose, and my family and I became inspired by it.

Although I had reached the finish line of my first cancer battle, there was still a long way to go. I would return to Memphis for frequent checkups. Even though my doctors knew the cancer was gone, it did not necessarily mean it could be gone forever. Due to the possibility of recurrence due to other diseases, doctors did not consider a kid cancer-free until five years after going into remission.

In the first year of checkups, I would return every three months. After a year, I returned every six months, and then a year after that, every year. When I first returned, I would have to go back for about four to five consecutive days. After the first couple of years, it would go down to only three days since specific tests and scans were not in my appointment schedule.

The time I was back there for the checkup days involved many tests and scans (blood tests, a positron emission tomography (PET) scan, a CAT scan, a magnetic resonance imaging (MRI), and so on.). Along with the tests and scans, I had appointments with cardiopulmonary services, speech, physical therapy, eye clinic, dental clinic, and whatever clinics my doctor felt were necessary to see if there was any sign of tumors while analyzing the side effects of treatment. Despite the day being almost full of appointments, it gave me and my parents a chance to see all the doctors and nurses who had taken care of me during my treatment once again. After I finished all my appointments for the day, we went out to explore areas outside of the hospital.

One of my favorite activities was when my parents took me and both of my sisters to Libertyland Amusement Park. The park did have a handful of roller coasters, but it also had various typical little kid's rides, making it a great trip. The park sadly closed its doors permanently years ago, but I will still be forever grateful for the experience I got there. Another memorable trip was the entire family (myself, my mom, my dad, and my sisters) going on the Memphis Queen Riverboat ride down the Mississippi River. The boat is huge, with dozens of areas to sit on and chill in, but what makes it such a wonderful experience is the possibility of seeing the different regions in Memphis.

The most heartwarming experience was when we went on a "Memphis Carriage Ride." It has not been my favorite activity to do in Memphis. Still, it was a touching experience because we again saw another family that we met at Ronald McDonald House during my treatment. They were beyond happy to see us again, and we were grateful and glad to see them. It was another great reminder of the part left behind in Memphis, but this time, it was with no sorrow, just straight happiness, and laughter.

Not long after I went into remission, the Make-A-Wish Foundation reached out to me and my family. Make-A-Wish is a nonprofit organization that grants wishes to children living with life-threatening illnesses. Since I had just finished my cancer treatment, I was eligible to receive a wish through them. We received a letter through the mail explaining who they were and the lead team member's contact information. To help achieve my desired wish, Make-A-Wish assigned a group of volunteers called "the wish granters team" to me.

My parents showed me the available choices and, after some consideration and thinking, I decided. My parents, of course, did not want to influence my choice since I only had one wish. They still helped me choose the most memorable and best option out of all of them. As a kid, you want everything you can get your hands on, but Make-A-Wish had a policy restricting each child to one wish to make every dream come true.

Several days after I officially made my choice, the "wish granters" team and five volunteer employees from Lowes showed up at my house to assemble a middle-sized playhouse. The playhouse consisted of the central part, which had a set of stairs that led up to the inside of the playhouse. It had a giant swirly slide on the side that went out from the inside of the playhouse to the outside, and a little straight slide that came out from the inside to the back of the playhouse. The other part (to the right of the playhouse) had a strip of wood that hung three swings and a handlebar. It was more than I could imagine and something that became a better part of my childhood later in life.

In addition to the playhouse, I also was able to add an all-expenses-covered party at Chuck E Cheese in Davenport, Iowa. There are so many memories I cannot recall from my childhood, but I can never forget walking outside to see a limo in the driveway. I may not remember my exact reaction from when the limo drove up to the front door, and I walked outside. What I can say, though, is based on photos taken that day; I was both shocked and beyond happy at such a fantastic sight. I am sure few kids can say, "Yeah, I had a limo drive up directly to my door." It is a situation you would only see in Hollywood films.

Along with my parents, two sisters, and brother, I was able to bring a family friend and her two kids, which included one kid who was also going through cancer treatment at the same time. One of my aunts, uncles, and two cousins had also joined us for the occasion. Riding in the limo was everything you could dream of, and even more, especially with me being the curious kid I was back then. The time at Chuck E Cheese was a blast, and the fact I got the chance to share the experience with some of my family made it an exceptional experience. We played games and whatever other activities that we could do there until we became exhausted.

Through my chosen wish, I got everything I could have imagined. I may not have received the biggest, most expensive wish, but I got the experience I desperately needed after a rough battle. I endured days of feeling like the end would not come, and now those days were behind me and my family. Finally, I had seen the bright light. For the first time since my diagnosis, I got the true feeling of not being a sick kid anymore. Most importantly, I realized what it truly meant to be a kid again.

What made the experience so special was the "wish grant-ers team" coming together to make the wish possible, includ-ing the Lowes volunteer workers and the limo driver. They all dedicated their time and energy to making the impossible happen. It will touch my family and my heart forever. I may never see or hear from them again, but the magic they pulled together to make my wish possible will forever be with me. My gratitude will always go out to every volunteer for taking the time to impact my and my family's lives that day. Beyond that, I want to give extraordinary gratitude to the "Make-A-Wish Foundation." Because of the organization and my wish granters team, I witnessed how miracles can be possible when people unite.

During one of my previous checkups, my medical team at St. Jude brought up a concern I had thought would be in the past. Since my head remained the abnormal shape that it was when I had first arrived at St. Jude, they requested a licensed neurologist to check my head. Not long after our arrival home, my parents took me to my pediatrician, who referred me to a neurologist at the OSF Saint Francis Medical Center in Peoria. Even what the neurologist told us could not prepare us for the answer we wanted to know for so long.

He found, after analyzing the prior tests conducted and current testing, that the bones in my head had closed too early, which caused my head to be the shape it was. What I found hard to comprehend was how different the situation could have been. The neurologist mentioned how doctors should have addressed it earlier when the problem first arose. If a neurologist had addressed the problem early on, they could have scheduled a procedure to prevent the bones from closing too early, leading to my closer-to-normal head shape.

Due to the strong development of the condition, my parents had two choices. I could have surgery done, where the surgeon would cut into my brain, which would leave me with a huge scar that would go from one ear to the other ear at the top of my head. The other choice was for there not to be surgery done, and I would remain with the oddly shaped head for the rest of my life. As much as it hurt my parents to make that decision, they decided not to move forward with the surgery, which would eventually cause the bones in my head to close too quickly and, thus, would cause my head to be an oval shape permanently. They knew it came down to the choice of me having an odd-shaped head for the rest of my life or having a huge scar that would be easily noticeable, with the potential to cause even more problems later in life.

Am I mad at my parent's choice, even today? Not at all. I know it was not an easy choice to make. While I am not trying to justify their decision, in all honesty, if I were them, I would have made the same decision. The choice did end up leaving me with a noticeable odd body part, but it beats having to walk around with an embarrassingly large scar any day. They did not know it was a serious condition until it was too late. The neurologist told us back then that the only way they could have done a procedure without leaving a considerably noticeable scar was if the doctors caught it early on, so I do not and never blame them for the tough decision.

Besides the times I went back to Memphis for my checkups, life at home returned to how it was before. Only, this time, my parents had a child they watched over more closely than before my diagnosis. They did not treat me any differently, but they did make sure to occasionally (well, between checkups) take a double look over my body and some of my vitals to see if anything was abnormal. While my parents knew my cancer had vanished, the entire cancer experience did not stop them from worrying.

I returned to being the same kid I was before. I continued doing the same kid's activities as before and focused on what every child deserves: experiencing the growth part of their childhood. My entire family was grateful for me finally being back home with them. Except, this time, I made sure to make what I could out of life since I was bearing witness to fate almost taking my life away in a matter of seconds.

With me still only at about three and a half years old, I honestly did not have many friends. As I have mentioned before, though, one opportunity that came for my dad being in the military was all the people he met. He met a fellow soldier working at his National Guard location. He had a son named Jacob, who was interested in the same activities as me. To this day, I can still remember his mom telling me, "I remember the early days when you guys were next to each other in baby carriers." As our friendship grew, so did my mom's and his stepmom's friendship. One commonality they shared was scrapbooking, so on some days, they got together to do a scrapbooking session, or our dads would hang out, and Jacob and I would hang out.

Then one day, my life changed forever again. Just like my parents noticed me not crawling at about the age I should have; they also grew concerned about why I was not showing signs of speaking. As with the last time, they took me to the doctors, who then referred me to the Black Hawk Area Special Education District. After looking at the earlier evaluations at the Children's Hospital of Iowa and doing some more testing there, in April of 2002, I received a diagnosis of "Expressive Language Disorder." Due to my earlier developmental delay diagnosis, they said it was related to that condition, and nothing would change except for the fact that I would have to remain in speech therapy.

Later, in the fall of 2002, after turning four, I got closer to being able to attend elementary school when my parents enrolled me in a SKIP (Special Kids in Preschool) program back home. Due to my prior developmental delay diagnosis, I met the program enrollment requirements. The two-year program was a preparation course for children with learning disabilities, developmental delays, or any other disease that affected the way they learned. It taught whatever skills it could to pre-pare children for the best successes possible before entering kindergarten.

Specifically, with my inability to speak, the staff would use a book with pictures of various objects to help me commu-nicate. For example, I would point to a picture of what I was trying to say. So, for instance, if I wanted something to drink, I would point my finger to a photo with a cup in it. Although I did finally start speaking around age four, I continued speech therapy.

I would be lying if I said I did not feel anger or helplessness at the fact that I went through this program because of some-thing I did not choose to have. Not having a choice of being a kid with a developmental delay did impact me in a negative light. However, at the same time, not being the only one stuck in the same situation helped ease some of those emotions I started feeling. After the end of the program, there was a small graduation ceremony for the children who successfully passed the program. After the other children and I went through the program for two years, there was a graduation ceremony on May 28th, 2004.

# 5

# Unexpected Terminal

I already endured so much and realized firsthand what hopelessness looked like. Some might say that a few life events should not define everything going forward. However, when you go through a few early diagnoses after birth and a cancer experience, everything changes. I may not remember every day I remained in the hospital during my battle with cancer, but the emotions tied to that event and my early two diagnoses after birth in my life stayed with me after the treatment. I had just hoped it would be the end of the darkness starting to take a toll on my life.

As a family member of active military personnel, you never want to consider the possibility of the day the government calls them to serve. Most of my dad's army friends have at least served in one war (well, that I know of). No matter what thoughts you have going on in your mind, it does not help that it is bound to happen sooner rather than later. Around three years after going into remission, my family received more unfortunate news.

Several weeks into September of 2003, my father received a

call that the government had called up an enormous number of troops. The troops included the group of national guardsmen that he was in, to go overseas to fight in the Iraq War in response to the deadly 9/11 attacks. The following days were not normal at all. They consisted of my father packing and spending as much time with family and friends as possible. My father then left with his fellow brothers in arms to head off to training for about five months before arriving in Iraq in March of 2004.

We all knew that with our beloved support and God watching over him, he would be all right and protected. It did not help that anything could happen, especially once he was in an uncontrolled environment. As my father has always said whenever asked about heading off to any war, "You don't know what you are getting yourself into until you are there in that reality." On top of that, with already so many soldiers not returning home due to perishing in battle, it struck much fear in my family. Nevertheless, we still remembered all the guardian angels out there and knew they would be with us every step of the way, just as they had been during my cancer treatment.

Both my family and I felt an emptiness in the days following my father's departure. Even though we knew he would be good with it being just training for the moment, it was not easy. While it was not the first time my father would not be in our presence, it was the first time my siblings, our mother, and I would be apart from my father for that long. For the first time, my mother had to learn how to become both a mother and a father for the duration of him being gone. She had to learn to care for my siblings and maintain the house by herself while still working full-time.

It would not be the same around the house without my father, but the thought of him doing it to protect my family (and the United States) from outside harm kept our minds at ease.

I was not fully aware of what was happening back then, but inside, I knew that my father was doing life-changing work. While it felt like a lifetime, only eighteen months had passed for the soldiers being apart that were separated from their loved ones. My father and the other soldiers will never forget the day the higher army officers told them that replacements would be arriving to take their place, finally allowing them to return to their families. While it would still be a few months until the troops came back, the news gave so much hope that both the troops and the families needed.

March of 2005 became an unforgettable day. The buses with the troops finally arrived back at the Illinois National Guard unit. Many family members of each soldier stood at the front and by the sidewalk on which the soldiers walked into the building. Before the soldiers could return to their family's arms, the unit held a formation inside for the troops. As soon as the formation ended, my mother, my sisters, and I rushed to my father's side. He took my mother in his arms. The best part, though, was the giant smile on my father's face upon seeing his family for the first time in a long time.

The days following my father finally being back home were a big dream come true. We had the family back together, and I had my father, whom I could now see daily. We would not have to worry about him receiving another deployment call, at least for a good while. No matter what was going on now, we knew he was there to stay, and no feeling was better than that one.

Before we knew it, life started taking its own direction. I cannot tell you everything that happened moving forward because I was so young. And I do not remember everything. What I can say is the need for a change in my family was more vital. Our small house had become too small for all of us, and my parents wanted more space. There were a few other factors involved with a change, like when some unknown hood rat vandalized my parents' car, and the fact that my parent's friends were in a different town.

The answer was simple: move to a town about twenty-five miles away. The town was small, but it offered so much from more stores and significant opportunities. More importantly, it offered other possibilities while still offering the same quiet vibe we loved. On top of that, it was the same town my parents' friends lived in. The other positive note was that it was not too far from our family, so at least we could still visit as often as possible. My father particularly liked the idea since we would be in the same town as the National Guard, where he worked part-time.

After searching, my parents found a two-level house with five bedrooms, two bathrooms, and a two-car garage. The house had more space than needed, but my parents did not mind the extra space. A few months after my father returned home, we moved into the new house in the spring of 2005, which marked the beginning of a new chapter. Moving is always exhausting and not fun, but the new atmosphere and life undoubtedly made up for it.

With the move also came a new school for my sisters and me. We moved at the beginning of summer break, but my parents wasted no time signing us up for the next school year. My mother went to the school's office to get us signed up as soon as possible once we moved. The only downside that existed for me was how I would still have to continue receiving occupational, physical, and speech therapy at my new school.

The new experience was more than my family and I had expected. Not only did we get a new beginning, but a fresh start as well. On top of both, the town provided greater opportunities, such as making new friends at my new school and participating in soccer. I may not remember the main reason for deciding to get involved in sports, but I would say it was a mixture of wanting to try something new and my father encouraging me to find a way to discover more of myself.

It worked, though. I fit in perfectly (yes, even with the oddly shaped head and speech problem) with what I considered "the popular crowd" and found myself growing with new friendships and an activity I loved. Not only did I start becoming a normal child and forming friendships at school but I also in soccer. One of the new friendships I formed was with Trenton, whose mom was the other coach on the team we were on. We both shared similar interests, especially soccer, and easily bound like no one else. It led to a powerful friendship. While my parents and I enjoyed the new life, sadly, it would have its troubles.

My father's experience in Iraq remained with him despite the fresh start. Where darkness managed to coexist with the war in Iraq, the same darkness found a way back home with my father. Life changed despite him finally returning home with his family and friends. While some part of him remained the same person before his deployment, a small part of him changed. That was not the only part to experience a change as problems in my parents' marriage arose.

Like many couples, over the several months of living in the new place, they started becoming different while experiencing different thoughts on topics. My mother would think from one perspective, while my father thought from a distinct perspective. Before they knew it, they had just gotten to the point where they made the tough decision to file for a divorce. Not that they did not want to try to make it work, but even that might not have worked out. They just did not want to risk it with how the fighting started affecting me and my siblings. So, they decided to take it up in writing.

I would be lying if I said the divorce did not affect me. I may have still been young at that time, but it was apparent that something was up. I at least knew some despair was making its way toward me. I just feared what was going to happen to my parents when they officially separated. I felt helpless to the reality that the world was coming down, and I had no control. Though I knew I had to trust in God, and if that was the way it was supposed to work, then that is how it would be.

I really wanted both of my parents to stay in my life, and if that were possible, everything else would be okay. Despite my mother winning custody of me, my father chose to remain living in town. Therefore, he could once again help me in coaching my soccer team in the spring of 2007 while still seeing me as much as possible. Just because it did not work out between him and my mom, it did not necessarily mean he could not remain a part of my life. Even with the pain that ended up coming from the divorce, he still wanted to watch me grow and be there for me as a father.

Some might say that the whole reason my parents got a divorce was because of how life had become different after my father arrived home from Iraq. Although, this was not the case. The truth is that divorces happen all the time because couples experience different perspectives and grow apart. I am not saying his deployment did not play a role in the divorce, but it was not the main reason. Despite everything that had happened, including the new moving situation ending up turning into my parents separating, life in my eyes remained stable. I still had the positive experience of starting a new journey, and both parents cared about me. Plus, my father would be close to me.

# 6

## Second Round

The beginning of fall 2007 started as normally as it could. For once, everything formed into how I imagined it was supposed to. I was doing great in school. I enjoyed life as much as possible with my new friends and my family; I had both parents in my life looking out for me; and I found a piece of me through playing soccer. At that point, life became settled as it should have been from the start. Despite the obstacles I previously faced and being a bit of an outsider at school because of being in the special education program (with the regular classes) and continuing speech therapy, I started enjoying life while looking forward to the future.

Since the first year after officially hitting the remission mark, St. Jude had me return once a year in November. Since I was six years post-remission, this time, I did not have to do so many different tests. The only tests my doctors said were necessary were blood work and a body exam. To a doctor, once you reach the five-year remission mark, the possibility of cancer returning becomes slim, and there was not a high recurrence of non-Hodgkin's in survivors at that time.

With only a few tests, I could go to the Peoria clinic instead of flying to Memphis. It is not like we did not want to travel to Memphis, but with everything going on in my life, the convenience of driving about an hour versus flying to another state was better. My father wanted to go with my mother and me, but he could not tag along with us because he was scheduled to work that day. However, there was no doubt he would be the first person my mother would tell the test results to as soon as my mother received them.

We knew by heart that the same fantastic care offered by doctors and nurses would still be at the Peoria location. So, for us, there was no downside to going to the Peoria clinic for my checkup. We just hoped that we would go to the checkup for the doctors to tell us I was still in remission, but the facts of relapse in cancer survivors were obvious. Treatment does kill the cancerous tumors, but it still is an unfortunate permanent fix in some situations. Yes, some survivors are fortunate to live out the rest of their lives without the cancer returning; others are not so lucky due to all the genetic disorders and other conditions out there.

I do not have a complete remembrance of the full exact timeline from the point when we arrived at the Peoria clinic to when the doctors walked into the room to announce the unfortunate test results. What I do remember is that a tumor showed up on a scan ordered by my doctors after one of my appointments. Then, in the flash of a moment, I woke up after surgery with a large tube going down my nose and my family standing next to me with the same hopeless feeling as the first time my family heard the words, "Your child has cancer." A conversation with my mom held that thought to be entirely accurate.

During my body exam, one of the St. Jude doctors felt something strange in my stomach. He grew overly concerned and ordered me to have a CAT scan done right away. According to the doctors back then, the CAT scan showed a new tumor growing inside my stomach. The doctors did not want to believe it was my cancer returning. Unfortunately, the tumor was in the same spot as my first cancer battle, so they could not ignore the fact that it was my cancer showing its face once again.

Everyone in the room felt mixed emotions, especially anger, upon the news of the horrible reality returning to our lives. My mother felt upset, hurt, and mad that I would have to go through something like that again. My father shared the same feeling my mother expressed. He is a more emotional person, so he broke down even more when my mother told him about the news over the phone. I shared the same feeling as everyone else while now having an utterly broken spirit.

Being older than at the time of my first diagnosis, I became more aware of my surroundings. This time, I knew well what was going on and the misery coming my way. The doctors themselves were just upset with the unknown fact of why my cancer came back, especially with a cancer type that presumably did not return after successful treatment. Neither the doctors nor the St. Jude staff failed at their jobs; there was a different reason for the relapse. They cared so much for every child, and a child with cancer standing in front of them was devastating.

Despite the despair now in the room, the doctors were determined to get me back into remission. The treatment would remain straightforward like last time. Doctors would take as much of the tumor as possible in surgery, and chemotherapy would kill the remaining tumor. There was no doubt that the doctors aimed at getting the entire tumor taken out in surgery. However, that is not always possible in some situations. Since hospitals are busy, the surgery would not occur until two days after my relapse.

I do not know what was worse for me: the fact I had to endure a living hell again or the heartbreaking phone call my mother made on the way home telling my father the cancer had returned. As expected, my immediate family rushed right to me to hold me in their arms once I got home that night. They knew well the strong fighter I had become and that there was no doubt I would use it in battle. It just did not help with a good chance I would make it out alive, and they were already aware that the second time of having cancer is harsher than the first time. On top of that, even if I made it through, what would happen to ensure my cancer would not return a third time?

The next day, my parents had only two jobs; one was to ensure I was best prepared to make it out of the surgery successfully and then to immediately start contacting the rest of my family about the situation. It was hard enough on them the first time. For it to return left them speechless and in a tornado of emotions. If I remember correctly, I spent part of that day getting almost suffocated by many of my family members through hugs. I cannot blame them, though, because as far as they knew, it could have been the last day with me alive.

Before I knew it, the day for surgery came. With many of my family members working, only my siblings and two of my father's friends went up to the hospital with my parents and me. Walking up to the hospital and into the surgery prep room was the worst. I knew I would make it out of surgery alive, but it did not help that there was still a slim chance of the surgery not being successful. For my family, the uncertainty of the situation just ate them up inside. Nevertheless, they would remember God's wisdom and he would be with them every step of the way. While many family members could not physically be there, they made sure to call whenever they could to see how the surgery was going.

The elementary school I was currently attending was highly supportive that day. Many wore purple ribbons to show their support, symbolizing faith, hope, and love. Plus, my whole class signed a card and banner with their signatures with a get-well message. Even my parents could not hold back their tears upon seeing the card, banner, and two photos from my school. One photo showed the entire elementary school, and the other showed just my class, with the letters "We love Jacob" in both images. For my family and me, it was so heart-touching for many others to acknowledge someone else's despair in a time of need.

To everyone in the waiting room, that very day felt like a whole century passed by. However, only about three to four hours went by until a doctor finally came out to reveal the outcome of the surgery. Through God's grace, the doctors extracted most of my cancer, or as they pointed out, "a tumor the size of a baseball." However, because the rest of the tumor was extremely close to my bladder, doctors could not take out that part, which would mean chemotherapy treatment would kill off the remaining tumor.

While everyone was beyond happy about the part of the surgery turning out successful and me making it out alive, we all still knew a long road to full recovery lay ahead, minus whatever the remaining treatment ended up bringing. Oddly enough, I do well remember waking up in the recovery room, my family standing by my bed and not being able to talk because of the large tube I had up my nose. It is ironic to think about today, but I guess some events in life are so hard to forget, especially with me not having the ability to move or talk much at the same time. The additional thought of us wanting to know what had caused my cancer relapse ate us up more than anything else.

The following several days in the hospital recovering will always be the worst days of the whole ordeal. I had not yet faced the actual reality of being a cancer patient, but everything in my body wanted to give up desperately. Unlike my first round, a severe new problem came up. Precisely three days following my surgery, there was an infection in the wound where the tumors were. Nobody, especially the medical staff, could figure out how the infection had developed, but it did. While my medical team gave me a few options, the best choice came from having a wound vacuum and typical IV antibiotics.

If there is a product I could not ever seem to explain specifically, it is what a wound vacuum is. From what I do remember though, a wound vacuum is a device attached to the wound to remove any lousy tissue/bacteria and produce new tissue while allowing the wound to heal from the inside out. As with serious wounds, sealed bandages go directly on the wound, but unlike other wounds, a piece of foam is under the sealed dressing to suck up any tissue/bacteria, with a drainage tube connected to the dressing. Lastly, the other side of the tube goes to a suction canister, with a separate tube going to the suction device.

With how serious a wound vacuum treatment is, a licensed home nurse came on a scheduled day once a week when I was at home resting. During the duration of her visit, she checked on the condition of the wound while changing the dressing that the suction part sat on (so, in my case, it was my stomach). After looking at the current condition of the wound, the nurse would adjust the size of the foam as the size of my wound gradually decreased. Much to surprise, the dressing change was not extremely painful; it just felt weird. It was as if a doctor had cut my skin off and then stitched it back onto my body, but the area was completely numb.

My medical team decided on an accommodation where I

received a bag large enough to fit both the suction canister and the device. So, this way, I would only have a tube going from my stomach area to the bag. This still did not help because I would be stuck with this problem for at least two and a half months to let the wound completely heal. There are so many flashbacks that give me chills and get me into a pool of negative feelings to this day, but this memory will always be the worst one. I do not mean to make it sound so bad, but having to live for so long with the device and finding a way to sleep comfortably at night is one flashback I always hated looking back on.

As I have mentioned, though, the more brutal news came from the fact that I would again have to go through chemotherapy to effectively kill the remaining portion of the tumor. My medical team decided to schedule a procedure for a few days following the surgery for a central line to be inserted through my chest. Like the previous one, the central line would allow easy access to any IV liquids (including the chemo liquids) that needed to go into my body. This way, any licensed medical professional would not have to poke me a million times within one day.

The main advantage this time was the treatment location option, compared to the one restrictive choice on my first round. During that period, the clinic in Peoria became better equipped and updated with the latest medical technology. So, if we desired, the St. Jude Peoria clinic could provide the treatment. It was an easy decision for my parents, and they quickly agreed. It is not like they did not want to travel to Memphis, but doing treatment at the Peoria location was more convenient and flexible.

With me doing treatment there, my mother could still go to work as much as possible to keep my sisters and me supported financially. Plus, I would easily be able to go back to my natural home in between my treatments. My father, too, would have the same flexibility to work still while being by my side in the hospital as much as possible. More importantly, most of my family and friends would not be far away. So many of them would be able to drive up to see me during treatment this time instead of just a phone call.

As I mentioned, my family and I remembered that the same fantastic care offered at the Memphis location also existed at the Peoria clinic, so there was no downside. The family atmosphere between the patients and the patients' families was the same as Memphis. The entire staff treating the patients like they were their children existed there, too. To my parents, "The nurses and doctors at the clinic are so remarkable, patient, and caring." My parents quickly saw what I had seen in them myself and were just grateful for what unique human beings they all were. On top of that, at least by doing treatment there, I could see the same hospital staff I was getting close to through my previous checkups.

I honestly did not want to think about all the preparation that had to be done before I started my chemotherapy, but what I can say is that it was a handful. At least one of my parents had to fill out numerous pieces of medical paperwork along with meetings between the doctors and my parents to discuss the treatment. Most of all, both parents had to figure out stuff at home, especially my mom. Even though we would not be far away this time, between my mom working and being at the hospital, she had to still ensure my sisters would have everything they needed back home. A lot of it, though, really became my entire family still coping in a way with the fact I was once again a sick child with cancer. For me personally, to go from a life I was starting to love and enjoy to being a helpless, ill child was just an unbelievable nightmare.

One other problem my mother had to figure out was my schooling situation. I obviously could not go to public school due to the time I would spend at the clinic for my chemotherapy and whenever I returned to the clinic due to my blood counts dropping. My parents did not want me to miss schooling and be held back. After some discussions between the head staff of the school I was attending and my parents, they came to a solution. They had a few substitute teachers, so one could be available to home-school me.

My parents were open to anything, especially if the situation helped make life at home during my cancer treatment more manageable. However, there was no doubt that they both remained worried. To have a child without a learning deficit would have been no worry, but for me to be in an unfamiliar environment with my developmental delay terrified them. From what they knew, I would have easily adjusted, or it could have backfired in no time. Unfortunately, there was no other option but to go ahead and say yes to it.

I may not remember my reaction to her walking through the front door. What I can say is that knowing Mrs. Peterson through all these years; the experience was a fantastic one for my family and me. She is an all-around great, unique, polite person and teacher. She knew how to teach and educate any student effectively. The roadblocks in front of me, such as my cancer situation or my learning deficit, did not matter. She remained determined for me to continue my learning.

Most of all, she was patient with me and did not rush me. I could say she displayed this trait because I knew I was battling a severe illness, but it was not in any way, shape, or form. She had children, so she knew how to communicate with a child efficiently. She understood a child inside and out through raising her own children, which helped her succeed in her job.

What stood out to me the most was how I saw the same level of caring in her as in the St. Jude staff. She may have only come to my house a few times a week for the school sessions, but it was a time I looked forward to. To this day, I will be extremely grateful for her walking into my life.

During the sessions, she came over for about two hours. The communal areas taught in school, like English, Social Studies, Spelling, Math, Science, and History were discussed as thoroughly as possible. With only a few hours, Science and History had to become a minority to ensure she discussed the critical areas typically covered in regular school. It was not Mrs. Peterson, nor even I who wanted more time to go into the material, but with me battling cancer, sitting at a table for a lengthy period was not possible. At the very beginning of my treatment, it was not a problem to be up for a good period, but once the treatment side effects kicked in, it would not be simple. So, with the current circumstances of my cancer situation, a few hours seemed reasonable.

Then, before I knew it, the actual reality set in of me once again going through chemotherapy and becoming a child potentially on his deathbed. When I thought my endless days of the nasty side effects of chemotherapy and feeling like there was no clear road had passed, they once again began. I had no choice but to face the actual reality in front of me. I had to face the fact that I was a sick child who might have seemed strong on the outside but was still scared with so much uncertainty on the inside.

I was not the only one; many family members shared the same dreadful feelings. They faced those feelings but, unlike me, found an important lesson in those challenging times. A lesson to keep focusing on the good parts of that situation, such as having the best medical team I could have and my family being there with me. The lesson taught us that if you keep focusing on the bad, it will get nowhere except in a great ocean of despair. Nevertheless, if you keep remembering the good in the situation, you already know the meaning of hope and will come back on top no matter what steps in front of you.

This time around, some little aspects changed, which made treatment this time more manageable. Compared to the first time, I would be within close driving distance of many of my family members. So, this time, they finally got the privilege of coming to see me on the days I was stuck in the hospital. Whenever family members and either my friends or friends of the family could find time on a day off work, they would come up and visit me in my hospital room.

Even though it was not easy seeing me like that, they were still grateful for the flexibility of seeing me in person. With my father's dad and my father's mother living about one hour away from the hospital, they frequently found time to spend with me either in my hospital room or during one of my little checkups inside the St. Jude clinic. For my father to have his dad by his side throughout the ordeal became a blessing. It shows that, no matter how old we get, our need for support from our parents never disappears.

Even with the current situation we cancer patients face, we still look forward to the holidays, especially Christmas. I may have been a sick child, but I could not help but smile during the Christmas party St. Jude held in the clinic in December 2007. Once again, I forgot the horrible reality and enjoyed what normal children enjoyed back home. Food, laughter with family, and presents from Santa. From what I remember, I had a vague list, but the three remote toys, Legos, Nerf ammo balls, magic rocks, and the bird feeder were more than I could have imagined. For me to enjoy times like these just lifted my spirits so much!

Like the first round, this time was no different in the side effects that came with chemotherapy. I will never forget about three weeks into my treatment when the chemo drugs wiped away my hair cells, and I officially lost my hair. I knew it was coming because it was not my first rodeo, but it did not make it any easier. It is crazy to think someone losing their hair is not a big deal, but in a way, it is. For most people, hair is a part of their personality, and with it being a part of their appearance, it can impact someone if they lose it. I just remembered that it was a temporary situation, and eventually, I would have my hair back!

Along with the hair loss from the chemotherapy came more side effects like fatigue, nausea, loss of appetite at times, and, worse of all, low blood counts. Whenever my blood count dropped below five hundred (which happened frequently), I would immediately start running a fever. So, either one of my parents or both had to take me to the St. Jude Peoria Hospital. With your body being weaker during low blood count levels, an infection can happen more quickly. So, antibiotics had to be administered through my central line to keep infections away. The upside to hospital stays is the visits from various generous, caring people. Individuals and groups, including musicians and sports teams, would visit the patients. One of my favorite moments was when former White Sox designated hitter and Peoria native Jim Thome visited the hospital. I may not be a White Sox fan, but still, for me to meet a professional baseball player is a memory I will always treasure!

That would not be the only time I would return to Peoria between treatments, as I went back to the St. Jude clinic twice a week for a mandatory status update. Besides the now usual chemo rounds and the mandatory check into the St. Jude Peoria hospital for low blood counts, along came the times I went back to the clinic for the doctors to check up on the progress of the treatment. Some days, the progress check would last only a few hours, but on the days that I needed platelets or a blood transfusion, I would be there for the entire day. There was no way out of these visits, as it is just the actual harsh reality of a cancer patient.

The days I spent the entire day in the clinic would be decent. The waiting room had different stuff to keep me busy, along with the staff's activities for the patients. Some days, I would play games like *Guitar Hero* on PlayStation Two, play rounds of pool, or sit and relax. It was nice that my family was just a short distance from the clinic. Many would join me and my parents for my checkups. Along with either or both of my sisters, my grandpa would come up whenever possible, too, so I always looked forward to beating him in a round of pool! I also, without a doubt, looked forward to the other different activities. To this day, one of my favorite activities was when I learned how to make slime.

One common space I spent as much time as possible in the hospital on my better days was the children's life room. Numerous activities for a kid to do were in the room, including toys, video games, and arts and crafts. Art may not be my favorite subject, but to us patients, it was still something to do and took our minds off our cancerous reality. Even with me not being the best drawer (I mean, I never was!), I would often draw basic pictures. Oddly enough, a few days after I drew something, I received a letter in the mail informing me my rainbow drawing was on display in the "Hospital's Children's Art Gallery." To this day, I will always continue to look back on this and how this one little bit of news lifted my spirit.

What became special to me was the bond that formed between us patients. There was no doubt it had remained the same fantastic experience as my first diagnosis. As strong as the bond between our parents was, the bond between us was more vital. None of us had the same looks, personality, interests, etc. It did not matter, though, because we all were children trying to overcome a severe life-threatening illness. Everyone knew what we were against and wanted to be there for each other. A lot of what led to such a bond is the days a fellow patient tried to cheer me up when I experienced a challenging day of not feeling good and then returning that same flavor to a fellow patient experiencing a dreadful day. Over time, we all became a giant family, and I will forever be grateful for having the experience of battling a horrible disease with those people.

On the various days I did have to return to the St. Jude clinic for the treatment status update checkups, I went through many tests for at least a good portion of the day. Everything typically at the beginning of a regular doctor's checkup, plus additional testing to see if the tumor had been either growing or sinking. Lab work, checking my stomach area, and sometimes testing via PET, CAT, or MRI scans became my new norm in these checkups. Sometimes, it was a lot of different tests, but I needed to go through the necessary tests so each update on my treatment progress was as accurate as possible.

I did not mind them since I had already grown to treatment status checkups from my first round. Neither my family nor I became opposed to them because we wanted to know if the treatment was effective or not. I would say, though, that the number one test I hated and made my jaw drop was the CAT scan. I could not care less to do the scan itself, but the contrast was a different story. The taste of the contrast was (and still is!) by far the worst liquid chemical that has ever gone down my throat.

It became so gross and intolerable to me that I would get

sick and throw up every time it went down. For the longest time, I thought throwing up from the chemo was the worst but throwing up from the nasty CAT scan contrast easily outbeats it. It did not help significantly because it was such a large amount. So, after a brief time, I started refusing to drink the contrast. However, with this test being so important, there was no way I could not go forward without it. Yes, the blood work showed some of the results the doctors were looking for, but the CAT scan showed a visual representation of the inside of my stomach that blood counts could not deliver.

Oddly enough, I still remember a bit from a meeting with the doctors to discuss options to get the contrast down. What I do remember is figuring out a puzzle and looking up at an image of a nasogastric (NG) tube while my parents and doctors sat and talked. As I said, the test had to be one way or another, and since I was not drinking the contrast, my medical team told my parents that the last resort would be a licensed doctor putting the tube through my nose. The end of the tube (so the end part that hung outside my nose) would have an open port for the syringe with the CAT scan contrast. The liquid went through the tube and inside my body. By any means, I did not want that object stuck down my nose, but I also knew drinking the contrast was so awful. And so, I just decided to suck it up.

At least by that time, I already knew what it felt like to have a strange object feed through my nose. The difference this time was that I would have to experience the uncomfortable feeling of the tube going through my nose and to my stomach area, all while conscious. Having to be awake and listening to the doctor guide me, especially the part where the doctor told me to swallow, so the tube could get past the Hypopharynx, will always be another unimaginable memory. Getting the tube inserted was not fun, but it beat having to drink the nasty contrast. I was already growing tired of throwing up from the chemo, and throwing up from the CAT scan contrast was an unbearable nightmare.

Between my chemo rounds, going back for treatment status checkups, and frequently going back from my blood counts dropping, the clinic turned out to be my second home. The life I had started to build back up became a memory of the past. In a flash, I once went back to being a sick child with cancer. This time, I had more of my family there supporting me every step of the way, but with all the time I spent at the clinic, it was hard to remember my actual home.

I cannot lie, though, and say that I never looked forward to returning to the clinic and seeing the staff. Every single staff member brought an instant smile to my face. They would even often make me forget my cancerous reality when I stepped into their presence. In a way, when both my family and I stepped into their presence, it felt like a weight lifted off our shoulders. To this day, I know that if it were not for them, the hope of me overcoming my cancer would not be possible in any way. I keep talking about this like a broken record, but it is hard not to talk about people who have profoundly impacted another person's life.

What I would say, though, was eating up both my family and me at that point was finding out the reason for my cancer returning. We all knew there was a reason for my relapse, and we wanted to find it out desperately. The focus was no doubt on getting the remaining portion of the tumor gone, but at the same time, finding out the reason for my cancer relapse was important. I mean, even if treatment once again killed the remaining portion of the tumor, what if there was no guarantee of it returning a third time?

During one day of my appointments, a St. Jude nurse drew

a blood sample from my mom, my dad, and me. My medical team at St. Jude wanted a sample from my parents so researchers could test it for genetics. The test would give my family and me the truth behind my cancer returning after six years when it was not supposed to in the first place. With how much time the various tests take, there was no confirmation that researchers would discover the answer behind my relapse even within a week. As much as the anticipation killed me, I would rather have time for the tests to be run successfully than make a mistake because of me being impatient. I mean, was it not better to be safe than sorry?

Several weeks after my first day of treatment, the doctors discovered the reason for my cancer relapse. Still, even with the answer we were all seeking, nothing would prepare us for the despair that came with it. Through intensive research, my doctors found that I inherited an X-linked lymphoproliferative disorder called "Duncan's Syndrome." Due to my mother initially being a carrier, they instantly connected the dots to her passing those genes down to me, which had caused Duncan's Syndrome to develop inside my body.

The harsh reality of having that disease is now taking more than chemotherapy to get rid of the disease and return to remission. I would have to go through a treatment called a bone marrow transplant, which involved a specific set of days of higher chemotherapy drugs to knock out my current immune system completely. Finally, on the tenth day, one of the nurses assigned to the transplant floor would inject the new bone marrow cells from my anonymous donor through my IV, giving me a new immune system and blood type system. Following the tenth day, I would have to endure several months of the most challenging recovery period anybody could think of.

The bone marrow transplant would be unlike anything I

had faced before and was something I never thought I would have ever had to face. When I was already close enough to the ground with the current treatment, the transplant would put me directly at the edge of death's doorstep. Worse of all, the bone marrow transplant was a 50/50 shot, so either I would come up on top or end up buried in the ground. I would be facing my most enormous life-or-death situation, with this one not in a way entirely in my hands. What would be especially hard with this decision for both my parents and me was the possibility of me not surviving the transplant. The most heartbreaking part about the news was that, without the transplant, my cancer would come back a third time. But this time, I would not survive it due to how much more aggressive it gets every time a patient's cancer returns.

The following days were the most challenging of my parents' lives. They shared anger, fear, hopelessness, and heartbreak deep in their hearts. They were facing the most challenging decision, especially for them once again reeling on strong hope. My mother felt tremendously torn about putting me through it. My parents wanted me to get better so much, but at the same time, they did not want to lose me.

Sometimes, it takes hearing another person's perspective to think about the situation in front of you. Like any night my mom worked, she often talked to her co-workers during some of their downtime. Similarly, as with my family and friends, they would frequently ask about how I was doing, particularly about the status of my cancer situation. There was no doubt she enjoyed the bond she and her coworkers shared.

One night at work, she told a coworker about how I needed a bone marrow transplant and that if I did not get it, there would be no guarantee that my cancer would not resurface a third time. Every concern both my parents shared, particularly with not wanting to lose me, she shared. Her co-worker understood the matter-of-fact going through with the transplant. Though at the same time, she realized deeply the negative consequences of me not receiving the transplant. She understood my mom's hesitation due to not wanting to lose me.

She once again explained that counting chemotherapy only for my cancer to return a third time would not be worth it. She said that even though surviving the transplant was not a guarantee, I needed to go through with the transplant because of the high possibility of a cancer relapse without the transplant. To put it best in her words and get it through my mother's head, she said, "Are you thinking more about yourself than what's best for your son?" While my mother still felt conflicted about the decision, she could not deny what her co-worker told her.

After discussing it with my father and sharing the perspective of her coworker and them both once again thinking about what the doctors said, a few days later they went to doctors. They agreed for me to have the transplant done. In thinking about the transplant, they just came to realize the toll a third cancer battle would have taken on all of us, particularly with the strong possibility of losing me. They both witnessed how aggressive my cancer became the second time and did not want to witness its wrath again. Even with the slight possibility of me not making it out of the transplant, they knew it was the right decision in the end. I deserved a chance to live a life without having cancer again. It was not the easiest decision to make, but they knew it was the right one.

# 7

# At the Edge of Death's Door

Following five months of chemotherapy, the hope my family and I needed shined our way. After finishing the last dosage of chemotherapy, I was once again in remission on March 24, 2008. For everyone, hope prevailed in ways we did not know were possible. By no means did we believe it was not entirely over yet; though for me to be able to declare victory for a second time brought positive feelings everyone deserved. We all had been stuck in an ocean of despair for so long, and when the doctors walked through the door to announce the update, we all were speechless.

I won the battle, but the war was far from over. There was no turning back once my mother had agreed for me to go through with the transplant. It indeed was not negatable once I went back into remission. If the transplant did not happen, I would have to face the certainty of my cancer coming back and taking my life next time. To back out would put my future at severe risk. I knew deep in my heart the choice we all had to agree upon; the transplant. I came too far along to give up and not finish the entire battle.

Even today, I cannot remember a longer wait than until I could finally receive the transplant. Compared to the simple paperwork and admission to the hospital for me to receive chemotherapy, there was a lot more to do before I could go to the St. Jude Hospital in Memphis to undergo the transplant. I would have to go to the Memphis location a few times. Once there, I would get a handful of stuff done outside the standard paperwork. The first time would be to have various tests done via bloodwork, scans, etc.

With the chemo associated with the transplant being high doses, the doctors needed to ensure both my body and my blood counts were in the best condition possible. The second visit would be to have dental work done. Anything to make sure my teeth were in the best condition, including good cleaning and fillings, and from what I remember, one of my teeth was pulled by the St. Jude dentist. The next visit would be to do the final paperwork, testing, and detailed discussions with the doctors about the transplant.

Unfortunately, before those visits could occur, a donor had to be found. Without a healthy donor, there was no way the transplant could be possible. After all, high-dose chemo made up only half of the transplant. My mom was not qualified because she was an X-linked lymphoproliferative disease (XLP) carrier, and my father was not a match. So, we had to turn to the donor registry. There was no doubt a single family member or family friend would not hesitate to donate. Still, there was no match. The donor registry became the best option because I needed a match as quickly as possible. It would ensure I made it through the transplant.

Around this time, another problem occurred. My parents started to struggle with the costs outside of my treatment. With generous donors always supporting St. Jude, the donation money covered all the costs associated with treatment. Therefore, no family would have to take on that specific burden. However, the costs of gas, plus everyday expenses back home for my parents' places, turned into a significant burden. My parents wanted to be with me at the hospital so badly, yet they had to make sure they took care of themselves financially, especially with my mom taking care of my sisters.

Neither of them would mind working more, but their main intention of being with me through this tough time was a priority. Both were already working as much as possible and neither wanted to give up being there for me because of having to be working all the time. Sadly, neither could ignore the pile of adult bills that came their way. Over time, though, people around us became aware of the growing costs.

Not a single person hesitated to step in to help with the growing expenses and share their support. Not everyone could give us money directly, but it did not stop them from finding a way to help my case. My great friend, Trenton, did something on his part that completely blew away everyone around me, especially myself. He learned of a $1,000 contest named "Oprah's Big Give," which received a local portion sponsorship from a TV News Station in the Quad Cities. The contest aimed for people to give away their money to worthy causes. He went to his mother and expressed extreme interest in winning the money and handing it over to my parents to help with the ongoing expenses. "I want to win the money for Jacob so he can get better and return to school," he told his mother back then.

Immediately inspired by his simple gesture, she wrote up my story and sent it to the Quad Cities news station. She did not have a big plan. Rather, she just explained my current challenging situation and how her son wanted to help me in any way possible. His submission caught the eyes of the station, who was touched by Trenton's generous gesture. Trenton's submission also won the hearts of the contest judges. An employee from the news station called his mother to inform her Trenton had won and become a finalist for the $5,000 additional prize. Surprisingly, we were unaware of what he did until we went to Trenton's place one day. At first, I thought it would be a day for us to hang out as usual. Before we could get into hanging out, he informed us of his submission of my story into the contest. Best of all, a few employees from the television station had stopped by to drop off the cardboard-style check upon his win.

My parents and my own heart stopped upon him telling us the news. For Trenton to do something so kind was heartfelt, and my parents and I were so speechless. It was hard to describe the feeling. "It takes a special person to do what Trenton has done," she later expressed to the station's news crew. For Trenton's reason for his submission, he said, "If it was the opposite and if I was sitting in the hospital, he would do the same for me," and he was not wrong! He went on to add about how our friendship was the primary influence for his willingness to win the contest for me.

What we did not expect was what would come next several days later. Like the previous visit, Trenton's parents invited my parents and me to their place, but this time, my brother came with us. I wondered if there was something more, and sure enough, my curiosity quickly got the best of me. From what I remember, I could not stop staring out the living room window. When I managed to get distracted and stop looking, the station live news van drove into the driveway. We learned at that second that, with a fantastic miracle and a generous number of votes, Trenton had won the additional $5,000.

We could not believe the miracle before us, especially when

we desperately needed it. For everyone, especially everyone who voted for Trenton, to come together and do something meaningful brought all of us to tears. The whole news station crew got out of the van to go live during the 5:30 pm newscast to surprise Trenton and me. Everyone did live interviews with all of us. To look back at this is amazing. It is amazing to think of how much of an impact a community can have on a person, and to be on TV is an experience that my family and I will never forget.

Around the same time, the elementary school I was attending before my cancer relapse decided to raise money for me, with the end goal being to match the cash Trenton won. Some might say that the generosity of his help through his submission of our story to Oprah's Big Giveaway Contest was enough itself, but for him, it was the opposite. He wanted to do more, but that is just the outstanding person his parents raised him to be. Trenton had gone to one of our class teachers and asked if the whole class could get involved in raising more money.

Like the others Trenton reached out to, she felt touched by the gesture. She decided to talk to the principal to pitch the idea of the whole school getting involved. The principal decided to hold a contest to see which class level could raise the most money, with the winning class receiving a pizza and a swimming party at a nearby hotel. He wanted me to improve and would do anything to make that reality possible. The contest ran for over a week, which was not a long time. Still, the abbreviated period quickly seemed reasonable with everything else we needed to do before the transplant.

Fundraising efforts moved quickly. Money from birthdays, Christmas, allowances, chores, and so on went towards the contest. Before I could blink my eyes, so much unity was born at that very time in my life. Everyone thought about the bigger picture and realized the need for someone's miracle. Was I supposed to be mad for the generous gesture before me?

To close the contest, my class walked from the elementary school to the local community bank, pulling a wagon with jars of collected money. With my health status at the time, I was not certain I could join them until my parents saw how I was feeling on the day the walk happened. Much to my delight, the day of the walk was one of my good days, so I immediately declared my intention to walk with them. The walk may have been one of the longest walks of my life by far, but to be with my friends and classmates again was so fantastic. It once again felt like the normal times that existed before I got sick!

Without a doubt, my class won the contest by raising almost $1,300. Including my class part and a generous donation from the bank, the total ended up coming to almost $5,000. No one was surprised at the outcome, particularly my family and me. My family and I already witnessed the magic that can come out of people uniting for a more significant cause through our experience at St. Jude, so we were not surprised at the fantastic outcome of the contest.

On top of the contest outcome, two of the town's residents and businesspeople donated a pair of bicycles. There was one for Trenton and one for me, which one of the bank workers presented right after announcing the total amount raised. For someone to go out of their way to do something meaningful was heart-touching to everyone in the room. I really could not thank enough every single person involved in that great miracle.

The fundraising did not stop there, though. A few weeks after the end of the school contest, a benefit took place. Everything from an auction, a food bake sale, and craft stand, took place to raise as much money as possible. Above that, my family had a custom shirt shop design unique T-shirts, which said "Pulling for Jacob" in letters on the front with a wagon below it, and "We're pulling for Jacob" in letters on the back, with all people/groups involved in the fundraising efforts below. The custom shirt shop also made separate shirts for Trenton and me, which had the same design on the front, but on the back, it said "Thanks for the Pull" in letters with a picture of Trenton pulling me in a wagon.

On top of the fundraising efforts, the Mississippi River Valley Blood Center set up a booth to test for a donor match. My family knew it would be a long shot for a family member or friend to end up being a match. Even if there was no match for me, there could be a match for someone else who needed a donor. However, with only a limited time, we remained open to anything besides the donor search on the donor registry. On top of everything else, a few local musicians performed a set, with a special appearance by Mrs. Peterson's son-and-daughter band, Motorbiscuit.

We all did not expect the generous gift the band gave me. Before playing a song they had written for me before the show, the band gave me a guitar signed by all of them, plus a guitar case and a small amp. I was just shocked and so happy at the unexpected gift! Before the event, I was not interested in learning how to play an instrument, but sometimes, an incredible blessing comes your way.

Sadly, even with the fantastic turnout of my benefit, no match for a donor through tests by the Mississippi River Valley Blood Center came up. So, we would have to wait for a donor through the donor registry. Even though a donor match for my transplant was cold, I was happy with the outcome of the benefit. Everyone around me united for a more significant cause than themselves, and I could not think of anything more impactful than the unity that everyone witnessed that day. For my parents, "It was so heartwarming that people care." Like me, my parents were touched by the tremendous generosity shown to us at my benefit.

A couple of weeks after my benefit happened, I was set to go back to St. Jude for about a week to go through the first set of tests and discussions in preparation for the transplant. The search for a donor was still cold, but the staff at St. Jude wanted to start getting the preparation stuff out of the way so that when a donor came up in the donor registry, the transplant could happen as soon as possible. Since my father could not make it down there on the first trip due to work, a good friend of my family and her daughter joined me and my mom. We decided since they were joining us, we would drive down there.

The nice part about returning this time was that I got to stay in the "Memphis Grizzlies House." The building opened in 2004 for former patients returning for checkups or for new patients awaiting a spot in the Ronald McDonald House. For any patient/survivor child who needed housing for one to seven days, patient services would assign patients and their family to the Memphis Grizzlies House. The building was not as massive as the Ronald McDonald House but still had everything a hotel room would have to accommodate the children and whichever two family members stayed with them. Compared to the hotel I had stayed in before, this place was within walking distance of the hospital. When we did not feel like it, there was a scheduled shuttle bus that drove there and back to the hospital.

The building had (and from what I know, still does) sixty-four hotel-style rooms and thirty-six suites, with the regular rooms having what a hotel room would have. Areas on the first floor include a dining room area, a vending machine in a small room by the dining room, a living room area, and a couple of different playrooms for the children. My favorite area back then was the small basketball court, which is located on the left side of the outside of the building. Whenever I got a chance, I often shot hoops to pass up time.

The Memphis Grizzlies House staff would hold events for the patients throughout the week, so we looked forward to any events while we were there. One popular event they had was Domino's Pizza nights, which I always looked forward to! The unique part was that the same family atmosphere in the other St. Jude buildings was also there. Every patient/survivor staying in the building felt an easy connection to other patients/survivors through their past and their unique experiences at St. Jude. Even though all the patients/survivors had gone through different circumstances, we all still felt the impact left by our battle. Consequently, we, along with our parents, had become bound by it.

What was especially helpful was the row of rooms at the front, off to the left of the buildings for patients who needed isolation for however long. The rooms were so that any patient with a minor illness, like the flu, would not be close to the rest of the families in the building. To keep the other St. Jude families safe, they had to remain in the room until they were not contagious anymore. The rooms were like the regular rooms inside the building but had a modification. The room had a typical two-bed hotel room, but all the rooms had a second small lounge room attached. Every one of the lounge rooms had a table and a small sofa in it.

I will not go into the exact details of everything I had to do at the hospital during the three days. Like my previous checkups, I went through a wide range of tests and scans, with some one-on-one between us and doctors to talk about the transplant. The sole purpose of this visit was to see the shape my body was in and to ensure my counts were where they needed to be before I could go through the transplant. We also found out what the transplant entailed precisely.

For ten straight days, I would receive an extremely high dose of chemotherapy, which would kill off my current immune system. On the tenth day, one of the licensed nurses on the floor would inject the new bone marrow into my body through my central line. This procedure would also make me feel the worst I have ever felt and beyond worse than my chemo rounds before. In simpler terms, I would feel like a semi hitting and running over me repeatedly. We still one hundred percent knew I had to go through with the transplant, and there was no option.

After spending about two weeks back home, I returned to Memphis in June of that same year. This time, along with the routine talks with doctors about any updates about the transplant, St. Jude scheduled a separate appointment in the dental clinic. The dentist worked on everything from regular cleaning, teeth pulled, fillings, etc. The high-dose chemotherapy would affect me a lot, especially later, having a significant impact on the health of my teeth. With it only being my mother and me this time, we quickly decided flying would be easier.

I have always been a flying enthusiast. It is easy to understand many people's fears about flying with how far up you are, but that has not bothered me. I always thought it was due to the safety of being in an aircraft and not in the sky randomly floating. Now I know how flying lets you see more of the world in the sky. If you have been where I have been before, you will quickly understand my perspective. It is a new, unique perspective I learned to cherish despite the cons of flying in an airplane.

Like my previous visit, we would still be there for the same duration. I travel there one day, go through about three days' worth of appointments, and travel back the next day after the last day of my appointments. Then, a similar cycle repeated of us returning home for two to three weeks before going back for another visit. July of that year, though, marked my last visit before returning and remaining in Memphis until I became well again after the transplant. At that time, the doctors hoped we were getting close to finding a donor. So, they told us on my second visit back that patient services would arrange for us to be in a different St. Jude hotel building for the few weeks before my transplant happened.

This time, my father talked to his boss. He was able to join my mother and me. After my parents talked about whether to fly or drive down, they decided the best option this time was to travel in a car. Neither my mom nor my dad minded flying, but with it being the last visit before remaining down there for so long, having access to a vehicle would help us be able to do any activities. As sad as it sounds, for all we knew, it could be the last time all three of us were together down there before my potential early demise. We all especially wanted the option of having a vehicle to go out and enjoy Memphis after my appointments.

While I would still have some tests done, the main reason for this visit was really to go over the final details of the transplant and to make sure all the arrangements were suitable. Unlike my past treatments, the transplant involved some different circumstances. In all honesty, I expected it because of how different a transplant is from just chemotherapy. I would stay in the hospital for the whole countdown, plus the many days it took until I became well enough.

For the first time, we all learned of a transplant unit on a separate floor in the Chili's Care Center section of the hospital. This part of the building was solely for patients going through a transplant. From what I learned; the floor is the same as any hospital floor with rooms. The enormous difference is that this floor has more restrictions, particularly with the number of visitors on the floor, and different protocols set for the medical staff. After it became clear to the doctors that I was well and in stable condition, I would stay for the first part of my recovery period in a different St. Jude hotel building called "The Target House."

Despite all the St. Jude housing buildings being for numerous St. Jude patients, there is a slight difference among them. St. Jude decided to greenlight the Ronald McDonald House and the Grizzlies House (currently called "Tri Delta Place") for short-term lodging. Meanwhile, the Target House came about for long-term lodging. St. Jude patient services would assign a family there for any patient going through long-term treatment or a transplant. The advantage of staying in Target House was the two-bedroom apartment-style rooms (bedrooms, living room, kitchen, bathroom), which allow patients like me recovering from a transplant some independence. With the transplant making my immune system so vulnerable for several weeks immediately after finishing, I needed somewhere I would be more isolated from others. However, unlike the Ronald McDonald House, the visitor's policy at the Target House is stricter.

As I have said before, the transplant called for way different circumstances than that of chemotherapy, which became the main reason I stayed in the Target House. With my immune system being vulnerable, I had to avoid catching any bacteria in my body, which could quickly get me sick and make my body reject the transplant. We also needed somewhere my parents would have access to a kitchen for ourselves. This accommodation was possible since every room in the Target House has a full kitchen, including cookware and silverware.

On top of that primary protocol, there were others put in place for one year after I received my new bone marrow to ensure that I would not be back in the hospital. One huge change I had to adjust to was being unable to eat anything (and I mean ANYTHING) that could grow bacteria. The list including fountain drinks, cold meat, any sandwich meat opened for a specific amount of time, and so on. Worst of all, I would have to take several different medications following the transplant to help avoid getting sick quickly and help my body heal.

The upside to the Target House is like the Ronald McDonald House: the downstairs features play areas for all the families. Along with that feature is a playground and pavilion area with a couple of grills in the back. The building has an exercise room, laundry rooms on every floor, a craft room, and a large dining room inside the building. My favorite activities recalled from my memory are the numerous times I went down to play pool and all the bingo nights I attended.

The only downside to going out of my room is wearing a mask, but if it meant I could feel less alone and be in the presence of others, I did not mind. As much as we wanted to stay in the Ronald McDonald House, it was impossible this time. Looking back now, I am glad I stayed in the Target House. This way, I received the unique opportunity to experience all three St. Jude Housing facilities!

Then, for the final time, after several discussions about my post-transplant protocols and the final tests, I returned home before returning to Memphis for the transplant. After being home for several weeks, my mother got the long-anticipated call. The registry had found a match! Unfortunately, the registry could not give us any information on who they were and where they were from. What my family did know was that we were just highly grateful the registry had found a donor. Soon I could get back to being a normal child again.

Initially, my medical team scheduled the transplant to take place sometime between October and November. But somehow, my donor caught a common minor cold and was sick. Since I had to wait until he was completely healthy to have the bone marrow taken out of him, my medical team moved the transplant to January 2009. Nevertheless, I would still only get a certain amount of time before having to return to Memphis in early October.

Before I knew it, the time for me to go back to Memphis for the final preparation period and the transplant had come. Both my parents and I traveled down to Memphis, and once again, in a way, I felt like I had become an actual patient again. With it taking about a week for the staff at the Target House to have my room ready, I would stay at the Grizzlies House, which was no problem since I had already loved staying there. After about a week, we finally moved into the Target House. I had never seen a place as big and beautiful as anything else. It felt like heaven, with so much hope and happiness.

The few months before my transplant involved testing, particularly a lot of different vitals being taken to make sure my counts were where they needed to be for the transplant. After appointments, I kept myself busy, whether it was an activity I could do in the lobby or my room or even exploring Memphis further. I brought my PlayStation 2 and PlayStation Portable (PSP) this time, so having my gaming consoles with me was incredible! Surprisingly, I did not spend much time on my gaming consoles. Often, I went down to the lobby or outside frequently, especially when I went out to shoot hoops at the Grizzlies House.

With playrooms in the Target House lobby and an outside playground, it became hard for me to stay cooped up in my room. My favorite things back then were pool, Pac-man, and playing outside on the playground. The significant part of this time was the fact that I was not experiencing pain. So, enjoying it out there in comfort and not as a sick child became a huge blessing for the moment.

Going to Graceland will always top any other activity I did in Memphis. Numerous places near the hospital offered free admission or discounts to every St. Jude family. So, we took it when my parents learned of getting free admission. Sure enough, the former home of the king of rock and roll did not disappoint! I cannot say if seeing the inside of Elvis's private plane or inside his house was better. The entire location is unique. Seeing some of the artifacts he once used was the icing on the cake and made the whole experience unforgettable.

One activity I never got tired of when I did feel good was when I spent time with one of my friends I met at St. Jude. Whether it was us doing something at the hospital waiting area, the Ronald McDonald House, or finding an activity not far away from the St. Jude campus, we always found something to do together. While my stay this time was at the Target House, I did have a few friends who resided in the Ronald McDonald House. So, I found myself going over there to hang out with them. My favorite memory is the time when one of my friends and I went to a monster truck event. The trucks were undoubtedly loud, but I took any opportunity to take my mind off the upcoming transplant.

There is one unforgettable memory I will never forget, which happened while I was down at the hospital in the few months before my transplant. My mom and I had gone to the cafeteria to grab food during a break between my appointments. Just like the other times, she would sometimes talk to one of the other patients' parents. While I was eating, she talked to a fellow patient's mom, who was sitting by herself right next to us. I could not hear every word of what they were talking about; what I noticed was the grief and sadness on her face. Later, I learned that her daughter had lost her cancer battle and had gone up to heaven.

To think about what happened to her was so terrifying. To me, it just was heartbreaking to hear someone so young could fade away, especially when it could have easily been me during either my first or second round. I know God does what he can, but sometimes, decisions are not in his control. It is how reality is. It did not help at the same time; I began to doubt my fate in going through the transplant. What if we were staring at the same fate that I would face while going through my transplant?

As much as neither my parents nor myself wanted to think about a dark thought such as that one, we could not deny my possible fatal outcome of my transplant. At that point, though, we knew we all just had to remain committed to the thought that I was going to get through the transplant and come out on top. We all knew what we signed up for as soon as my parents agreed to have the transplant done, and so we had to stick with it. The feelings associated when my cancer came back the second time, leaving all of us with so much insecurity that, without the transplant, I would for certain face a fatal relapse. None of us wanted to live that way, though, so deep down inside, a transplant was the only and best option.

Not soon after, I experienced the most extensive life-changing experience: Halloween and Christmas rolled around the corner. It was the perfect timing because of my and my parents' need for positive energy, especially as I got closer to my transplant date. With how big many of the events were while ensuring the safety of the children in the actual hospital, St. Jude often held the events at the Danny Thomas/ALSAC Pavilion.

For Halloween, a masquerade event took place. Me being the Star Wars fanatic I am, I decided to dress up as Darth Vader. Target House generously held an event at the same building for Christmas. The Target House mascot dog also made a special appearance during the event, so that patients could take pictures with him. Having the opportunity to take a picture with him back then was just fantastic!

My mother, as always, really missed my sisters and my family. I missed them as much as she did. The staff at St. Jude understood the situation. They offered to fly me and my parents back home for a couple of days for Thanksgiving and a few straight weeks for Christmas. Then, we would return for the transplant. With my counts and all the tests looking good so far, they saw no problem in me returning to see my family. They were not blind to the fact that it could even be the last time my family back home would see me with my eyes open. So, given the circumstances, they wanted to grant my wish to see my family for one last time before my life would be in hope's hands. A few days following the discussion, my parents and I flew back to Illinois for both holidays.

When we got home, I spent as much time with my siblings and family on both my father's and my mother's side of the family. My mom held our Thanksgiving family dinner for the family at our place, while one of my aunts hosted our annual Christmas family dinner at her house. My mother, too, gave separate time to my father for both holidays. Therefore, I could spend time with his side of the family. Following the time spent with my family, my mother and I drove back to Memphis to settle back in the Target House for a few days until we had to go to the transplant unit at the main St. Jude hospital.

Unfortunately, an unexpected circumstance prevented my father from being there while I went through the transplant. My mother assured him that she would call him to give him updates. With us being gone for a lengthy duration, another family needing housing moved into our room in Target House One, so patient services moved us to Target House Two. Both Target Houses were the same, so all the exact features in number one existed in number two. We were not missing anything, and I would still get to stay in the best St. Jude housing building available.

After a few days of rest at Target House Two, one of the St. Jude staff members assigned me to room seven in the transplant unit at the Chili's Care Center on January 13th, 2009. That same day of checking into the transplant floor, I started the ten-day chemotherapy countdown of my transplant. As I have mentioned, during those ten days, one of the licensed nurses administered various kinds of chemotherapy to kill off my immune system. The terrifying reality this time was receiving a higher dose of a chemo drug. Who knew what effects I would experience during the entire ten-day period? Even all the discussions with the doctors before the transplant still could not prepare me for what I went through during those ten days.

The first two days pretty much felt like my previous chemo rounds. I could feel the chemo hitting my body, but it neither drained my energy how I thought it would nor struck me as I had initially predicted. As the eager kid I was, I frequently got up to do an activity inside my room throughout those days. A good portion of my energy stayed intact in my body, so I made sure I was not a lazy kid.

There was not a day from the third day on that I did not

vomit, if not at least once, more than once throughout the entire day, every single day (well, until I reached day ten). In previous treatment, I would throw up sometimes, but this was different. I would frequently vomit throughout each day. It reached the point within the third day and after where I always kept a small wash basin close to my bed all day. So, when I vomited, it was in there and not on my clothes. The chemo then started striking me on the inside. It became hard to get up and want to move around. There was no doubt that, in the first half, I had enough strength to get up and move around somewhere. But then, it still became more difficult after a few days.

My sleep routine became unordinary after day three as I slept randomly throughout the daytime and nighttime. There was no exact time I fell asleep at night due to uncontrollable circumstances. Everything from me thinking enormously about the thought of potentially being on my deathbed, the noises from the medical equipment, a nurse coming in to check my vitals, or a nurse coming to insert medicine into my IV impacted my sleep. All the circumstances just made it harder to sleep during some nights.

One specific chemo drug, unlike the others, went through my body but exited through the pores of my skin. So, to prevent the chemo from leaving a permanent burning mark on my skin, my mother had to wash my body down in the bathtub in the restroom portion of my room. She had to do it every four hours on the dot for precisely twenty-four hours. If there were a time it felt as if the world were spinning, those twenty-four hours would be it.

On top of those conditions, the higher dose of chemo made me feel the most fragile I have ever felt. Without a choice in faith, I experienced the most hopelessness I ever felt in my lifetime. I went from being on top of the world to a broken-spirited heart child with an endless amount of despair. If there had been any time when I could not hide my agony. This time would have become an exception to it. As much as I tried to avoid showing that my body was not in the best state, it was not possible. I once again felt what every cancer patient felt upon extremely intense treatment: a sea of great despair and unimaginable rage. At the end of the day, though, I had to be strong and show I would reach the victory lane.

How I ended up getting through all ten days of the high-dose treatment will always be beyond me. Going into the transplant with a fifty percent chance of survival and feeling like I was on death's bed has only made me realize that miracles do exist. I know the stronger fighter and my willingness helped me get to day zero, but I also know that God being there and guiding me every step of the way made my victory possible. I can tell from my experiences and a friend who has had two transplants that God is there and with you during some of those very dark times.

Finally, after the ten severely challenging days, I reached day zero of my transplant. It was time for me to receive my new stem cells. I would not be kidding if I said I was as ready as possible but so anxious. Like my chemo, a licensed nurse inserted a medium-sized tube containing the liquid stem cells directly into my central line port. I officially received my new stem cells on January 23, 2009. From there on out, right after the last droplet, it would just be a waiting game to make sure my body did not reject the new stem cells.

Nevertheless, I would still have to remain in a rough recovery phase while I waited for my new stem cells to start producing on their own. The more challenging part may have ended, but not knowing whether my body would accept the gift drove me crazy. It did not help that, despite reaching day zero, I still had a long road of recovery to go toward rebuilding my health system entirely back up. The worst part of it was that I could find the part of me that managed to fade away in my battle against childhood trauma so far. I needed to claim the light at the end of the tunnel that paved a straight path for my life once before, and the only way I could do it was to rediscover hope.

*Me in my S.K.I.P graduation gown/cap with my diploma.*
*May 28th, 2004*

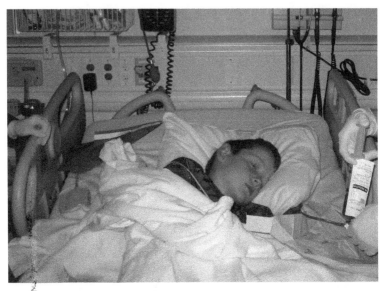

*One of the nurses injecting my bone marrow stem cells for day 10 of my bone marrow transplant on January 23rd, 2009.*

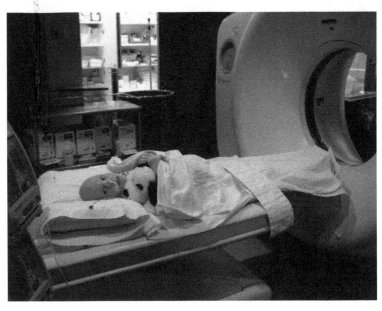

*Going through a CAT scan and holding a stuffed animal given to me in the hospital. All while trying not to think about the tube inserted through my nose for the CAT scan contrast. Taken during my second cancer battle.*

*Me playing (well, attempting to play) my electric guitar given to me back at my benefit in my Target House room before the transplant.*

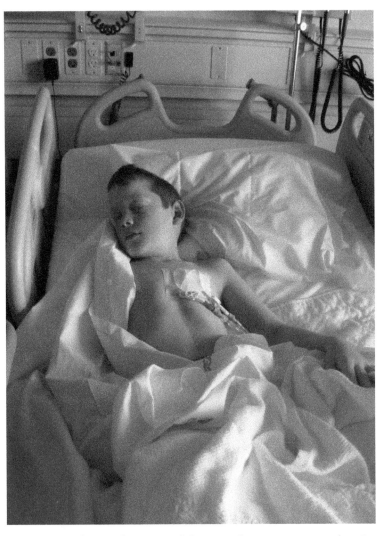

*Nap time during day seven of the transplant. I meant it when I said the high-dose chemo made me extremely tired!.*

*Making losing my hair following my transplant easier.*

*Me next to my handprint on the wall in*
*Ronald McDonald House during my first cancer battle.*

*Holding one of the items auctioned off at my benefit.*
*Taken during my second cancer battle before my transplant.*

*The message Keith Urban left on my hospital door when I met him.*

*Basketball time at the St. Jude Grizzlies House during my transplant preparation period in fall of 2008.*

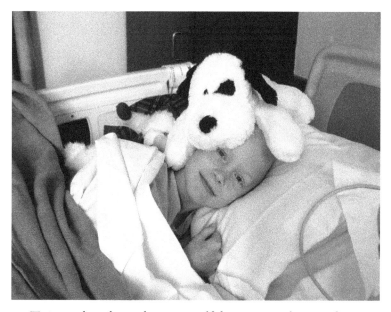

*Trying to keep hope alive in myself during a tough time of great adversity. Taken during my second cancer battle before my transplant.*

*Me next to my brick at the Ronald McDonald House during a checkup after the completion of my first cancer battle.*

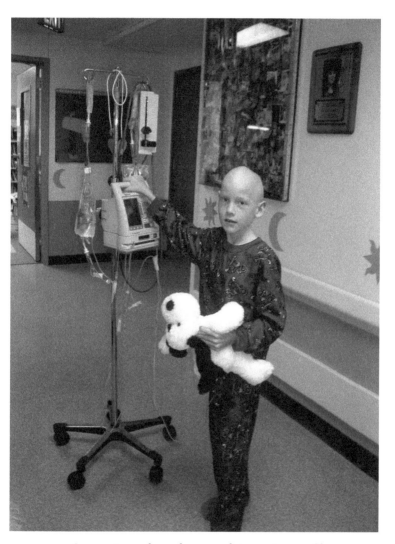

*Attempting to keep the strength intact in myself
during my second cancer battle.*

*Items given to me by the St. Jude staff after the completion of my first cancer battle (2003).*

*Items given to me by the St. Jude staff after the completion
of my bone marrow transplant & right before my release
from the hospital (2009).*

*The playhouse made possible by the Make-A-Wish Foundation several weeks after the completion of my first cancer battle.*

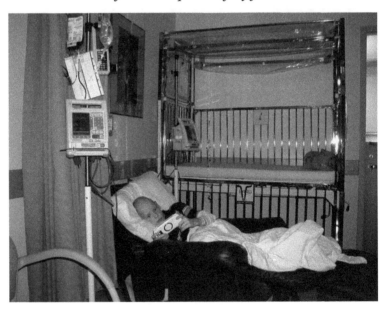

*Playing games on my PSP while receiving a blood transfusion at the Peoria St. Jude Clinic. Taken during my second cancer battle before my transplant.*

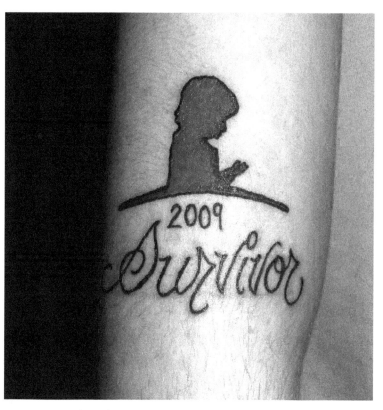

*Picture of my first tattoo right after the artist finished it on March 20th, 2016.*

*Opening presents during Christmas of 2009 while wearing
my End of Treatment T-Shirt the St. Jude staff gave me for
completing my bone marrow transplant.*

*Me next to the photo that I drew, featured in the St. Jude Hospital's Children's Art Gallery. Taken during my second cancer battle before my transplant.*

# 8

# Rough Healing Path

Usually, for a sizable number of cancer patients, once they finish treatment, it is not too long until the staff discharges them from the hospital. However, receiving a transplant is a whole new ball game. For the first five weeks following the day I reached zero of the transplant; it was different circumstances. I would remain in the hospital until it became clear to the doctors that I was stable enough to return to Target House Two. At that point, I barely had an immune system, so I understood well why I stayed in the hospital until at least a small portion of my new immune system grew.

The main advantage of my daily life going forward during my transplant recovery period was that I would not be vomiting as much. It still did not help, though the recovery period would be challenging. This phase of the transplant was rougher due to the changed lifestyle to which I would have to adjust for a year after day zero of my transplant. The plus from now on, though, was the free time I would get from not experiencing severe fatigue from chemotherapy.

To pass my free time, I would play the Wii (old Nintendo

console), board games, watch TV, and so on. I took up whatever I could get my hands on to keep me occupied. This time, it was not to make myself forget about my unimaginable current reality but to get to where I was before I underwent the transplant. I did not become lost entirely, but the turmoil from my whole relapse made my old self slowly fade away, and I wanted to find that person again. I just needed to keep reaching down to pick up the person I once was with the life and identity I once loved. Sadly, though, I could not deny that progress would not happen overnight. Rather, it would happen over time.

With the free time I got from not sleeping a lot, I did a handful of activities to regain the strength that the transplant took away. The various activities included physical therapy, speech therapy, breathing exercises, and daily visits from a teacher in St. Jude's personal schooling program. Additionally, doctors would periodically stop by my room to update me on my progress. Even with the first few rougher days following day zero of my transplant, I slowly started to feel better each day.

If there was one part of the transplant that was killed off for a good period, it was my appetite. Attempts to get me to eat solid food were unsuccessful, and I entirely stopped eating. It was not that I was hungry, but solid food did not taste the same for a while after the transplant. I would feel nauseated when I tried to eat. The food did not taste good. Even with different nausea medications, I still found it challenging to eat.

However, with food being crucial to staying alive, I had to get it in my body somehow. So, as a last resort, my medical team decided to put me on total parenteral nutrition (TPN) for nutrition. For anyone who has no clue what TPN is, it is a liquid mixture of nutrients and vitamins put directly into your vein or administered through a central line, as in my case. In my own words, TPN is a liquid food that serves the same purpose as solid food, giving the nutrients a person's body needs to function. It is undoubtedly a weird way to consume food, but the stomach needs its goods at the end of the day.

One experience I will never forget was when country music star Keith Urban walked into my hospital room right before my hair started falling out. Back then, my musical tastes were all over the place. Although I did listen to some rap music, I often listened to more pop music. Over the years, I listened to some country music here and there. Unfortunately, country music just has not become my cup of tea though. However, meeting any famous person, especially Keith Urban, will always be a unique, unforgettable experience. With some window markers, he even left a get-well message on one of the glass walls in my hospital room, which was very cool!

If there is one commonality between most cancer treatments, it is that the treatment often kills a patient's hair cells temporarily. Around a week after my transplant, the time came for my hair to start falling out. It did not end up bothering me at all. I immediately decided to help avoid making a bigger mess and pulled the remaining hair out. With my current hair cells now dead, all my hair particles came out easily and left no pain, making me lose my hair temporarily tolerable.

The support and motivation to keep pressing on every day, given to me by my mother and the entire St. Jude staff, did not change at all. I cannot count the days I hesitated to get up and get out of bed. Nevertheless, both my mother and the St. Jude staff worked tirelessly to find a way to get me up and moving. They all just ensured I saw the daylight and why I needed to improve. Therefore, I could return to a normal life.

What can I say, in this case? I was a child trying to cope with the trauma thrown at me so far in life while still traveling along a long, dark road to find the exact person I once was.

Not that I did not appreciate any of their support, but I lashed out in a way I should not have. The situation is an excellent example of how a dark situation can quickly get to you. However, after a while, I saw their view and started forcing myself to work towards improving. Even then, finding a way to further cope with my demons would be challenging.

Then, around Valentine's Day, I received a surprise. A family friend made his way down to the hospital and brought one of my sisters with him. If there became a time for a light to come my way, that would be the time. Since I made noteworthy progress and, most importantly, my body had accepted the new stem cells, the staff saw no problem in both people being in my hospital room. I became so happy with my sister by my side that I finally jumped out of bed for the first time without my mother or the medical staff interfering. Everyone around me could see how my mood had changed upon one of my sisters being by my side.

It did not help that there were only a few available activities. We saw no problem in the circumstances, though, and found whatever possible to do from board games, walking around the transplant floor, playing games on the Nintendo Wii, and coloring my hospital room glass windows. The other times were spent together talking and particularly enjoying being in each other's presence. Seeing one of my sisters again was more than good enough for the moment. With her being around, I found no excuse in saying there was nothing to do.

If there is one activity that I found myself turning to, it was watching movies if it was not music. Ever since I watched the 1994 movie *Angels in the Outfield*, I have found myself drawn to the storytelling aspect of the film. Before my relapse, I enjoyed movies on about the same level as the people around me. Between school, soccer, and hanging out with friends, though,

I had limited time to watch a movie. However, with the short number of activities available in my hospital room, I started to watch more films through the channels available on the TV in my hospital room.

During one night of watching some TV, the premiere of the Nickelodeon film *Spectacular!* changed my life forever. The film premiered on Monday, February 16th, 2009, only a few weeks into my recovery phase. Luckily, by then, I felt good enough to stay awake for the film's premiere on the Nickelodeon channel that night. To explain the entire film in exact detail would take a good while, but I will summarize it up for context.

The film portrays a high school rock singer chasing the dream of fame, particularly achieving that dream through a record deal. When he was chasing the dream through being in a band, he had the unexpected happen to him. He is kicked out of his band, which leads him to join a choir at his high school to win an upcoming competition and cash prize. Aside from him getting kicked out of the band, he endures several additional adversity roadblocks to achieve his battle, such as his brother not believing in his dream for a good duration of the film, trying to fit into the high school choir group, trying to make it in the extremely competitive music industry, and so on.

When I watched the film, for the first time in my life, I fully realized the similarities between the film's main protagonist and my battle to reach a great triumph. It not only resonated deeply with me but changed my perspective forever. By the end of the film, I had inhaled a new perspective through the film's protagonist determination and the willpower I knew I had deep down inside of me. Best of all, the film's themes of hope, determination, fighting for success, and the journey of re-discovery really resonated with me. Despite my hard work, I had started believing this battle would not be winnable. Worst of all, a small part of me almost lost hope that I would reach a great triumph in the fight. However, the film made me see that there would be a light at the end of the tunnel. And so, I had to successfully push through the challenging recovery phase of my transplant.

Most importantly, both of us had difficult obstacles thrown our way through our own battles with adversity. The only difference was that fate had not yet written the trajectory of my traumatic battle. The film made me fully see a perspective I never thought was possible. The perspective is that adversity does not ever define our story. Only how we overcome that adversity is what defines our story. A small aspect in seeing the perspective might have been the music part in the film, but I know it was the connection between my story and film's main protagonists that changed my life on that night.

After five weeks in the hospital recovering from my transplant, a new light finally came my way. All the medical staff working on the floor entered my room to commence the tradition, "No more chemo celebration." The staff chanted a "way to go" special song that the staff had created years ago, while a few nurses shot off a small confetti tube. The staff (like my first round) gave me an Extreme Makeover: St. Jude style t-shirt and a way-to-go poster board with a short message and signatures from every staff member that worked on the floor. Through the great miracle of modern medicine, all my counts reached a high enough level to return to Target House Two.

Tears of absolute happiness rolled down my mother's and my face when the staff started chanting the song. Best of all, the same feeling hit my father and the rest of my family as they learned of the news. I could not think of anything better than to start looking forward to going back to the life I had begun to build before my relapse. To hear from the St. Jude medical staff about the possibility of me living out the rest of my life cancer-free was a huge blessing.

We all were so happy; it was just indescribable. I still had a long road in front of me, but we all could physically see that I was in stable condition, and the tests just proved it. In a way, I was sad to leave all the generous staff on the floor who were with me in every step through one of the most challenging times in my life. At the same time, though, I was ready to start moving forward and fully find the person I once was.

A huge part of me felt a profound sense of rejoicing, but a small part of me felt a great sea of despair through more questions than answers and the most enormous burden imaginable: survivor's guilt. Why was I able to beat the disease not once but twice and survive a potentially life-ending transplant while other cancer patients suffered a different fate with their life? Why was my family left with complete hope while fate left their families with devastation for eternity? Why did God choose me and not any of the other cancer patients? Why was my life more important than their lives?

A part of me lay there asking myself some of those questions, plus more. I know to anyone, it would easily make me sound selfless to think about my victory that way, but I could not deny the despair now put on those families while fate had left me with enormous hope. Inside, I became consumed with the unanswered questions and left standing strong while other patients' fates ended with them going up to heaven. Meanwhile, their families were left broken. I felt what every cancer survivor feels upon hearing "you are officially in remission" in a matter of seconds.

On top of the survivor's guilt, the transplant would leave a forever mark on me through the more significant side effects.

For the rest of my life, I would be stuck with Vitamin D deficiency, left without half of my intestines in my stomach area, a case of permit eczema, and potentially many of my body organs experiencing unknown side effects later due to high-dose chemotherapy. With no other choice, I would have to take over-the-counter Vitamin D gummies and powered Benefiber to help control my bowels and various methods to control my eczema. On top of that, I would have to use an inhaler whenever I felt shortness of breath. The hardest part for me, though, was what worse side effects I could face later in life.

Among all the side effects I had to deal with for the rest of my life and my identity being under attack, it is not a lie that I felt so vulnerable to the life and world I once enjoyed. I slowly even started asking myself if I could face that reality now after I had gone through such despair. I could not erase any of the scars left on my body by the past two surgeries or the small circle scars left by where my central line had come out of my chest. I no doubt won the greatest battle of my life by overcoming my transplant, but the transplant had left me with a huge pile of unwanted consequences for surviving such an ordeal. I overcame the greatest adversity I could think of, but at what cost?

I wondered if I could find my way back to who I was and if I would find the normality I once grew to love. I endured many battles up until then, but going through the near-fatal transplant was unlike anything I faced. The transplant gave my family and me the hope we had been desperately seeking, but I would not ever be able to ignore the price tag of the transplant through the various long-lasting effects. For a reasonable amount of time, though, I had to remain hopeful and be grateful for the new gift St. Jude gave me.

I may never see every staff member working on the transplant unit floor again. Hopefully, if any of them are reading this by faith, my family and friends and I will never forget your commitment to help me overcome such a difficult obstacle. Like the other staff members at St. Jude, I know you were doing your job. Still, I will always know deep in my heart that you do it for a bigger purpose. The two items I will always treasure (on top of what St. Jude staff members gave to me in 2003) are the T-shirt and the signed poster board given to me by the staff on that very day. You all are a magnificent example of hope and unity. Please do not ever forget that unique trait instilled in you at birth.

I could go into detail about Target House Two, but with it being the same as Target House One, I decided to save some time. From what I know, though, only one Target House initially existed for long-term patients. The second Target House eventually came into existence after an influx of patients. As for me, I could hardly tell the difference between the two. Everything I typically did at Target House One I had also done at Target House Two, especially playing pool as much as possible. The nice part is that being in Target House Two had allowed me to meet more patients and their families while still enjoying all the different activities, including occasional events for the families, and any visit from the various St. Jude supporter groups.

While I struggled to sleep in a regular bed, it became comforting after several days. I knew deep inside, though, that I needed to get back to experiencing what was associated with a normal life. I knew not sleeping in a hospital room would help steer me in the right direction. Plus, seeing a more natural atmosphere at Target House Two gave me a better opportunity to start soaking in what my cancer tried to take from me. It gave me back what I slowly began to build before my relapse. I wish my recovery moving forward had remained recovering at Target House Two, but it could not be that simple.

Every day, including Saturdays and Sundays, I would return to the main Memphis St. Jude hospital for my daily appointments. I either went back to the hospital every single day for close observation and kept up with my recovery, or I stayed in the hospital all day, every day. Some days were short, but some were longer, depending on how many appointments I had for the day. During the time in the day that I was at the hospital, I went through a rotation between seeing my doctor, or going to triage to have my blood drawn. Sometimes this included blood transfusions, physical therapy sessions, and whatever other scans or tests my doctor ordered.

Most importantly, my doctor decided it was best to add frequent mandatory pulmonary function tests at the Cardiopulmonary Services Clinic to my appointment schedule to check my breathing patterns. For a portion of the day, though, I would go to the medicine room to receive IV medications to help my immune system return. Despite my white blood cells making quick progress toward rebuilding, for some reason, my red blood cells did not want to. So, the medicine room stops were always mandatory. The main reason for the daily appointments though, was to ensure that my new immune system was heading in the right direction.

Even with me not residing in the hospital, all the protocols set in place right after day zero of my transplant stayed intact, including me wearing a mask anytime I stepped outside my room at Target House. The one exception was either when I drank or ate something. Despite my progress, my appetite went to only eating a few bites here and there throughout the day. So, I still had to continue the TPN. We all knew my appetite would eventually return to normal, but it took longer than anything else within my recovery cycle.

The part I hated the most, though, and seemed more tortuous than anything else, was all the medicine I would have to take by mouth every day. I cannot recall the exact number of medications I took daily. I can say that by the negative memory it left, it was a good amount. The bad part is that, despite St. Jude's previous efforts to get me to learn how to swallow a pill during my transplant, I let my fear take over and did not end up becoming successful.

However, after my doctor spoke with the pharmacist, I did manage to get lucky with the liquid version for a few of my medications. The rest of my medications were still just the pill versions. My mother decided to help with some of the taste of the pills by wrapping the pills in a fruit rollup or another similar food. It did not ease the fact that they all tasted nasty, so the urge to vomit my guts out every single time one went down my mouth was very real.

I wish my daily life in the recovery cycle were simple and not so challenging. However, I can only get so many wishes in this life, and this one could not be one of them. Every day, in a small way, pushed me to my limits. I started to feel close to stable due to the considerable progress. Though with my immune system still not fully back, I could only get so far until I became exhausted. The vicious treatment was no longer, but the direct, immediate effects of the treatment, especially the weakness and fatigue at times, made my recovery right after the transplant had been so rough.

It was difficult to tell at first, but the doctors assured my mom and me that, as time passed, the stronger my body would get. Miraculously, it was believable a few weeks after my hospital release. Every day that passed I became stronger inside.

Before we all could believe it, a part of the child that once existed before my relapse started to find its way back slowly. Besides the time I found myself worn out from the various tests; I would find some activity to keep me occupied.

As before, I often went to the playroom on the first floor to play pool, whether with my sister, a fellow patient, or anybody who would say yes. Somehow, I sometimes got people from groups that visited us kids at the Target House to agree to play a few rounds. The other times, I found myself interested in the many activities held each week, especially the monthly bingo nights. Just enjoying a separate life outside a hospital room became tremendous. It allowed me to remember what it felt like to be a normal kid. I was not careless and kept up with everything put in place for my body's safety, but I could not deny the opportunity to see true life outside a hospital room.

The only missing piece of the puzzle was that the rest of my family was so far away. My mother shared the same feeling as me. She did not hesitate to express it to one of her friends one night when they talked over the phone. My mom's friend mentioned wanting to come down to see us and the St. Jude Hospital in person. Her kind boss understood the situation and let her take some time off to drive down. When my mother told me she planned to come down with my other sister and my young nephew, I stood speechless.

That weekend before Easter, I finally got to experience one of life's blessings that is often taken for granted. We were with more of my close family and my mother's friend. It may have only been me, my mother, my sisters, my nephew, and my mother's friend, but it was far more than enough for me. We did every common activity associated with Easter together, from coloring eggs and waking up early to see what the Easter bunny (well, our parents) brought my nephew and me.

Sadly, they had to return home a few days after arriving. We could not be upset because my mom's friend still had to care for her family back home. One of my sisters, who was already down there with my mom and me, had also returned with my mom's friend. It was a bittersweet moment, but I knew from my strength of getting better every single day that I would be alongside my family again before I blinked my eyes.

Nevertheless, I remained grateful for the brief time I had with them. If the surprise gave me anything, it was a more significant motivation to continue getting better. At about the same time as their departure on the morning of Easter, Target House held a celebration event for the patients themselves. They had an easter egg hunt on the main floor and gave every patient a small Easter basket. For me to still enjoy an exciting time despite my ongoing adversity was terrific. It made me realize some of life's small but unique blessings.

Before I knew it, my hard work of convincing myself to push forward had paid off at about the beginning of that May. The staff at St. Jude and my doctor gave my mother and me the news I needed to hear so much: my counts finally reached a high enough level that I could return home. Both my mother and I were beyond happy and blessed by the graceful news. When my mother called my father to inform him of the good news, he was speechless.

In a way, I did not want to leave all the staff at St. Jude and the Target House, but I was not blind to the fact that I missed everyone and life back home so much. Between being away from my beloved family and friends for so long and every obstacle I had to overcome with my treatment, it no doubt was a long, rough road for me. Deep inside, I had become more than ready, if anything else on the planet, to return to the life I had started building previously. At the same time, a small part of me was conflicted about my future and if I would find a clear path for myself. I had begun to build a life I knew well and loved deeply before my cancer relapse, but soon would find myself facing a greater darker adversity.

Unexpectedly, about a month before my departure back home, my nose started running like crazy, in addition to a low-grade fever. After taking a sinus-type test, the doctors found that, somehow, I had caught influenza A (aka the flu). Luckily, my immune system had become strong enough to fight it off by itself with the help of prescription medicine. Therefore, I would not have to go to the hospital. However, because of the other sick children actively battling cancer in Target House Two, my doctors made the immediate decision for me to stay in one of the isolation rooms at the Memphis Grizzlies House.

I stayed there for approximately three weeks to recover from the flu until the very day I headed back home. The entire time there seemed to me like I was staying in some inpatient psychiatric faculty but remembering it would not be too long until I finally returned home helped ease that thought. Partially, not having the choice to go outside made it a weird experience. At the same time, though, I liked having a bigger room than the Grizzlies House's regular room.

Any ride to St. Jude always seemed long; though the drive back home on May 12th felt so much longer than the nine-hour ride it was. More than anything else, I remained grateful I reached the most extraordinary victory I could ponder. A small part of me could not wonder if the same life at home and school would exist. However, I could not be selfless and let all the challenging work to get better go to waste. We got up early to head back to Illinois, and surprisingly enough, the weather was not bad. It allowed for a smooth, almost nine-hour trip.

As supportive as my hometown became before my

transplant, the same support remained there. We arrived back in town to see a message on the board of the gas station where Trenton's mom had currently worked. The sign read, "Welcome home, Jacob Mundy." On top of that surprise, I walked into my home to my sisters spraying silly string on me and a welcome home cake on the dining room table. Having so much support meant the world, but nothing mattered more than being back with my beloved family and friends. Thinking about all the visits from many of my family members and a few friends, along with seeing my father, which occurred in the days following my arrival home, was crazy.

I knew in my heart that I was right where I belonged. Nothing changed as far as the procedures set in place right after my transplant. Every single procedure, from my diet restriction, wearing a mask at any location outside my home, taking various medications, and weekly physical therapy, was mandatory for me until January of the following year. On top of all the continuous procedures, I would have to go to the St. Jude clinic in Peoria about once a month. Plus, I would have to go to the Memphis location every one to two months. Then, my doctors there could ensure my recovery was heading in the targeted positive direction it was meant to be.

I was deeply disappointed when I learned I could not return to school. However, after hearing why I could not return to school, my mood changed. As deeply as I wanted to return to school, I could not forget the associated risks that could arise. Thankfully, Mrs. Peterson could homeschool me and did not hesitate to say yes quickly. Besides, my homeschooling had been put aside for about one year until the medical team at St. Jude could confirm that my immune system had become strong enough to return to a regular school. In the meantime, life returned to how I hoped it did.

Apart from the rest of my recovery days, one day will always stick out, and certainly one I will never forget. Trenton came over to see me for the first time since I had left for my transplant. Following a few hours of playing and feeling perfectly fine, for some reason, I got sick fast. I started vomiting and running a fever. With how worried my mother instantly became, especially not knowing if it was my body rejecting the transplant, she called 911 to have an ambulance take me to the hospital. Moments later, an ambulance arrived to take me to the Galesburg emergency room. Once there, they calmed my symptoms down before an ambulance took me to Peoria.

By the grace of God, my recovery did not end up getting compromised. After an examination of my body and a few lab tests, the doctors at the St. Jude Peoria clinic found that, somehow, my central line had become infected. We do not know - and will not ever know - how it happened. It could have gotten infected, from one time my mom cleaned it, somehow something getting into it, or any other possibility.

For it not to be my body rejecting the transplant was a significant miracle. After the doctors talked to my mother, they realized there was no need for the central line to remain intact. After all, it had started becoming clear that the transplant was a success. Therefore, doctors decided to have my central line taken out. I stayed in the hospital for ten days for close observation and IV antibiotics to fully clear the infection. In a small way, it will always remain one of the scariest experiences of my life, but at least I no longer had the strange bump on my chest.

# 9

## Life Taken Too Soon
## (Interlude, part 1)

For someone to go through the awful experience of having cancer is beyond horrible. To go through watching a family member battling cancer will always be worse and a living nightmare. I will not know what exactly I did in life to have diagnosed myself with cancer. I will also not know the true answer to why life gave one of my beloved aunts a similar experience. About twenty-eight months after day zero of my transplant, my dad's side of my family found themselves in a heartbreaking situation. Unexpectedly, my Aunt Sue started experiencing unusual symptoms.

After going through several tests at a nearby hospital, doctors discovered that she had small-cell lung cancer. The horrific part was the fact that, unlike some other cancers, it was a rapidly growing type of cancer. The cause of the cancer was not one hundred percent clear, but from what the doctors could tell her, years of cigarette smoking could have played a part in her getting lung cancer. The doctors wanted to say everything was going to be all right. She would easily overcome it, but with her cancer type being a rare one, they could not give a clear answer to my Aunt Sue and her husband (my uncle) on a clear outcome.

Typically, doctors would suggest an effective treatment to kill the tumors. However, with small-cell lung cancer being a rare type of cancer, the possibility of a guaranteed effective treatment was not possible. The only option given was to go ahead and try some treatment, but even then, doctors predicted she had anywhere from thirty to ninety days to live. My Aunt Sue, being the strong fighter she was, did not want to go out without a fighting chance. And so, she agreed to at least try treatment.

She decided not to immediately tell my dad's extended family or any of her friends to protect my family. Some might say that decision was selfish, but looking back at it, I would disagree with that assessment. With the trauma my family had already gone through in my battle, my Aunt Sue and uncle did not want to put that weight on her entire family and friends. From what my father told me, he found out when he ran into another one of my other aunts on my dad's side of my family at the same hospital. That was where my Aunt Sue was getting help for her cancer battle. As much as she wanted to hide it, my father knew by her facial expression that something was not right. Thus, my aunt went ahead and told him of the unfortunate situation with my Aunt Sue.

After my father found out and informed me of the news, I felt utterly heartbroken. I felt so destroyed on the inside. It was not the same after my parents' divorce, but I always looked forward to seeing my Aunt Sue. I can always recall a time in my childhood when my father took me to her place for us to visit. She and my uncle made it feel like home. She cared so much about her family and for her precious gift of making her entire family feel like one of a kind, only to receive a terrible diagnosis that left all of us feeling devastated. To me, I could not understand why life left me to overcome cancer twice for my beloved Aunt Sue to be in a terrible situation.

Against all odds, my aunt's body did end up responding well to the treatment. As far as the doctors could tell, some of the tumors started to dissipate. Despite the progress she made with the treatment, the tumors grew faster than the treatment could stop. At first, just like my experience, the fact that she was battling a horrible disease did not become noticeable with a simple glance. Sadly, over time, the tumors grew in more areas of her body. Slowly it caused her body to deteriorate, and it became evident that she was battling an ugly disease.

However, if my entire family shares one essential trait, it is the willingness to keep fighting, even when we are faced with such adversity. It did not matter if the entire world was against us; we kept fighting. Unfortunately, there was only so much my family could do to help my Aunt Sue fight her cancer. What my family could do was hold a handful of benefit events to help ease the medical expenses.

In the following months, my family (with the help of my aunt's friends) held a few benefits, with every single one being successful. It became a different situation now. More people knew my aunt was sick, but my aunt and uncle knew they made the right choice in telling more people. It was not easy at all addressing my aunt's reality, but my family just realized this would not be a battle my Aunt Sue would win without the help of others. I wish her benefits were the bright miracle needed and would have solved the problem, but they only did so much. The treatment could only keep up with so many of the tumors, which led to her condition getting worse. My uncle then had to take her to the hospital just a few days after her benefit in October. She started experiencing seizures, and the tests showed no clear explanation of what was truly going on.

She ended up getting better and returned home a few days later. Doctors still could not tell what went wrong but she needed to focus on resting as much as possible. My family and aunt's friends held another successful benefit a few weeks after the incident. My aunt then got the call she deserved. Against all the circumstances, doctors said that scans she had done at the hospital showed everything was clear.

The situation did not take long to go upside down. Before long, my aunt experienced another unexpected seizure and fell. Following my uncle rushing her to the hospital, he called my cousin to tell him that he had taken her to the hospital. She had become close to unresponsive just a couple of weeks before Christmas. After a full PET scan, doctors discovered a tumor had gone up and attached to her brain, causing the sudden relapse. My father received a call from one of my family members about the situation. He picked up my brother and me to go to the hospital.

I felt utterly devastated when I walked into my aunt's hospital room and saw her in the hospital bed, barely able to respond. All while I firsthand experienced the same hopeless feeling my family felt in my cancer battle. Between the time I spent in my aunt's hospital room and sitting with my family in one of the visiting rooms by her room, it was the longest day of my life. Due to some circumstances, I left to go home to be with my mother that night. Now, thinking about it, though, a part of me ended up choosing to go home that night. I neither wanted to be at the hospital nor did I have any control over my aunt's fate while feeling hopeless.

December 28th of 2011 will always be the worst day of my life. My mother got off the phone to tell me my Aunt Sue had gone up to heaven. I felt like life ripped my heart out of my chest. A weight of rage on my shoulder escaped from not understanding why her fate turned out completely different from mine. If there existed a point in my life when I felt an enormous deep sense of survivor's guilt, her passing marked that point. Worst of all, I never received a proper chance to say goodbye to my Aunt Sue and it hurts. It will continue to hurt for the rest of my life. I chose to run away at a time that counted more than anything else, and it has haunted me for so long. Looking at the circumstances left in my aunt's battle compared to mine just made the experience so much more difficult.

If there is one memory that I cannot seem to remember fully, it is my aunt's funeral. If someone asked me to paint a picture of me being there, I would be standing. I still feel defeated and lost. However, nobody, in a way, could feel what my cousin felt following my aunt's death. For the first time, he would have to raise his two young daughters without the guidance of his mother. We all knew that as much as he seemed strong on the outside, he felt crushed entirely on the inside.

If you are wondering if the pain left following my aunt's death has become easier over time, ask one of my family members on my dad's side. They will tell you the same answer that I would say, "For anybody who says it gets easier over time, it doesn't." There is no doubt that at first, in a small way, life left both my aunt's family and me with a weight too difficult to bear. There is only life and death for every single person in this world, but when someone close to you dies too soon, it is a tremendous weight to handle. Over time, though, my family has learned how to move on without grief no longer getting in the way of the future.

We will never forget what happened, but that does not necessarily mean we should not continue living on. I know in my heart that my aunt would tell us we should live our lives to the fullest since we all get one shot at life. My Aunt Sue is not with us today, but that does not mean her memories and the time she had with her family and me are gone. We (your entire family & friends) will always love and miss you, Aunt Sue. Keep looking out for us up there in heaven as our guardian angel.

# 10

## Cloud of Uncertainty

The several months I spent working on my transplant recovery will always be the second most challenging adversity I have ever had to overcome. Every day upon returning home tested me more than I imagined. Between physical therapy and speech therapy, keeping up with protocols until January of the following year, adjusting to home-schooling, and returning to St. Jude for mandatory checkups, I questioned whether pushing forward would be worth it. Going through the near-death transplant left me with more inner strength than I could ever imagine, but missing what used to be and dealing with a dreadful recovery was a lot.

In a way, I just wanted to completely forget about my whole cancer experience. I wanted to return to a good, smooth life I knew I deserved deep down. I appreciated overcoming a life-changing situation that could have shortened my life, but with the circumstances left with my cancer situation. Because of it, I had become utterly conflicted. I felt like my entire world flipped upside down, and I could do nothing about it. All I knew was that I repeatedly moved forward one step only to take two steps backward. More than anything in the world, I just wanted not to be a kid cursed with trauma from my birth.

Finally, after a year of dealing with the procedures and the rest of my recovery conditions, my St. Jude medical team gave me the clearance to return to school in the fall of 2010. Since I stayed on top of my schooling while undergoing treatment and being homeschooled, I would return to the same class I was in and enter fifth grade with my classmates that fall. I was beyond happy when my mother told me I would not get left behind. Once I went to Memphis for my transplant, I became scared that I would end up falling behind. However, my motivation changed once I knew I would be returning alongside them in the same grade.

At that point in my life, there was no better time than after January passed. I no longer had to deal with incorporating the protocols into my life, and I had successfully beat all odds. I was back home where I belonged. Best of all, I was on the road to finding the person I once was before my cancer relapse. I would still return to St. Jude for checkups and continue physical therapy for a little longer, but at least those two bumps were less complex. I learned the hard saying, "You don't know what you've got until it is gone." When I got back, the few precious life gifts were being with my loved ones and eating traditional food. I was the happiest I had been in a long time.

As I originally predicted, my classmates welcomed me back to class with open arms. Not a single classmate of mine was upset by the adjustment of being back with them. It was a change we both had to adapt to after being apart for so long. Plus, now waking up to go to a classroom and not my dining room table for school sessions would take me a while to adjust.

My situation stayed the same for a good part of my school life. I stayed in a regular classroom with my classmates for some of my classes. However, for a few classes and my study hall period, I went to a specific classroom. I started going there before leaving for my transplant. It was designed for any child with a learning disability. The goal in that classroom was not to make us feel ashamed of our learning flaws but to put us in an environment where we had the necessary resources to succeed in school.

Due to me only making a good amount of progress before returning to school, my medical team at St. Jude decided I needed to continue speech and physical therapy at school. During a break between two of my classes, I would go down to the bottom level of the school to the school's speech therapist's room. Plus, my teachers and I would put time aside for me to work on many exercises assigned by a physical therapist outside the special ed classroom in-between classes. After thinking about how hard it would have been playing sports with my health circumstances, I decided to quit sports, including spring soccer, in next year's season.

I was not too fond of the thought of not playing soccer, but with my body strength not being what it was before my transplant. It would not have been easy after so long. Each time I thought about the decision in the following days, I found myself almost short of breath, especially when I did exercises in my PE class. I knew pushing my immune system beyond its capacity in sports to end up in the hospital would not be worth it. Soccer became more than a sport and would always mean a lot to me, but I had to accept the change. If I ever did return to playing soccer, I could not tell. However, I would always treasure the memories of playing soccer I had made, especially having my father as one of my coaches.

What I found most difficult was the change in my life. As much as I wanted to be a completely normal kid at school, it could not happen. The fact of the matter was that, when I left for my transplant, I had left behind more than I thought. I had left my normal life at school, the connection between me and a few of my classmates I became friends with before my relapse, and the person I became and grew to love.

Trenton went above and beyond in my time as a sick child, so there was no doubt our friendship would remain strong no matter what. The one question I could not stop asking myself, though, was if my situation at school would return to what it became before my cancer relapse. I had built a great life I loved at school in the years before my unexpected cancer relapse. Not knowing if my situation at school would return entirely to what it once was ate me up inside.

In the first few months of my return, life went back in the direction I had hoped. I started finding a way to reconnect with some of my classmates and working towards getting around the status quo I managed to build up before my transplant. Although I struggled to adjust to my new reality, I liked the idea of returning to a natural school environment. Everything at home and school was starting to go as I imagined.

Much to my dismay, though, my life at school later turned upside down. After a while of adjusting to going back to a regular school, my life at school did not end going back to what I once knew. It became apparent that the atmosphere at school adapted in its ways and was an environment I had no clue how to rip into after all. A few of my former friends found a new friend group and became a part of something I could not fit into solo. The only one at school still standing right by my side at that moment was Trenton and a small handful of my classmates. It seemed like most of my classmates had completely forgotten about me. I had returned only to most of my classmates to see me as a ghost, which made me an outcast.

Someone might ask why Trenton stood by my side. What I can say is I know he stood by my side because of the incredibly unique friendship we developed before my relapse. Someone who thinks less of another human being is not who his parents raised him to be. His parents raised him to be a genuinely caring person with sympathy and compassion for all human beings, and I know him having that strong trait led him to stay by my side despite my unfortunate situation at school. Trenton being there for me, though, could not help that school. It seemed as if I had left a place that now felt close to a complete ruin and a place to which I had started regretting coming back. I wanted the life I once loved at home and school to return, but only for my life at home to click precisely back into place.

The whole situation then started getting increasingly worse, leading to me becoming a victim of bullying. I fought so hard through my treatment so I could pick up where I left off. Yet, I discovered nothing but a cold, empty world at school. Worse of all, the few classmates who turned into friends before my relapse showed no interest in picking up where our friendship left off. They both found new friends in the group and set on targeting me as a bullying victim. While a respectable number of my classmates, as well as peers in the other grades, decided not to be involved in the hazing, it still did not stop the others from targeting me.

I would go to school every day being fearful of not know-ing what would happen. One of the first significant instances I can clearly remember is a former friend walking past my desk with the intent of letting his backpack hit me. Then, he took part in the negative gossip about me. I just felt so heartbroken about his unfortunate decision to forget our friendship. We had started becoming good friends before my cancer relapse, and for him to turn on me felt devastating.

After I told my mother what was going on, we both (along with one of my sisters) went to his place to talk to his mom. His actions towards me did end up calming down in the following days. However, I still could not erase the embarrassment of the confrontation encounter. He sure made it clear of the encounter at school. I only wondered if the torment would stop there, but it became clear the encounter had sent a clear message out to the rest of the school.

The message stated that everyone could mess with me, and there would be no repercussions. The message led to worse action at a school recess in the following several weeks. I had been walking around before deciding to take a quick second break to look at the sky while standing in front of one of the playgrounds. Then, a giant weight hit me in the flash of an eye, and I flew to the cold ground.

In a matter of seconds, one of the teachers took me to the school's nurse to treat my tremendous headache. They checked over the rest of my body for any potential injuries. From what I overheard; a classmate was playing a sport with our other classmates. He was running but did not see me, which caused him to bump into me accidentally. However, many classmates and I knew it was an intentional hit. The evidence of him playing a sport with our other classmates was clear, but there was no proof that he did not see me.

Another former friend who knew his statement was inaccurate stood up for me. While I was still in the nurse's office, he confronted him. I remember overhearing the confirmation later in the school day. He told him how mean it was to do something so selfish to another human being, especially since my presence there was noticeable. In his eyes and others, he told him that he easily could have avoided slamming into me.

I wish I could say that my situation at school improved

after the significant instance. Unfortunately, it did not improve; it worsened following the attack. From what I clearly remember, the instance was the last harmful attack for some time. That still did not stop the various dirty gossip or minor torment from going on. Some days, I would be lucky, and nothing would happen in school, but some of the other days became a living hell.

It also did not help that the atmosphere was different from what it had been back when my parents were in elementary and high school. When my parents were in elementary and high school, if a student were different, the other students would leave them be. Every student could go to school knowing they were in the safest place possible, and parents did not have to fear sending them there. The only similarity is that there was a popular crowd and one for the ones who did not fit in; however, the popular crowd always kept to themselves. When I was in elementary and a first-year high school student, the same two groups existed. Although, it became a norm for some popular kids to target the ones who did not fit in and make them ashamed of who they were.

Deep down inside my heart, I knew that the class that had once fought so hard to get me back where I belonged was still there. I could not deny, though, how the effect of the separation time between me and my classmates led to an unfortunate void. The truth was that we had both grown apart in separate ways during in our time apart. Different worlds came into existence in my world and their world. Many of the students found a way to take advantage of my skill of not being able to quickly adapt to society at school, including many of my classmates. While not everyone decided not to take part in the unjust behavior towards me, it still hurt deep down inside the ones that chose this.

The only good part that came from the significant incident moving forward in the rest of my elementary school years was a decrease in the bullying. In the following weeks after the attack, the only torment I would face was the negative dirty gossip going around. Most of all, though, there was a clear verbal indication by the mean group that I had become a true outsider. After completing my classes and the few years I spent with them, we returned to school to start our middle school years in a different building.

Despite the circumstances put in front of me on my return, I could not be happier for my school to hold an excellent eighth-grade promotion ceremony and a memorable celebration party by my mother. I worked so hard to reach this point in my life and enjoy it with the few faithful friends I still had. I was beyond happy once I finally got to the finish line in my earlier school years. The haters put in front of me may have tried to break me down, but in no way did they deny me this small life milestone.

I immediately thought the horror would finally be over once they cooled down during summer break. I did not know how wrong I would be, assuming the situation could turn entirely around after my eighth-grade promotion. As shocking as it sounds, the first few weeks back into my arrival in the ninth grade, the situation at school seemed like it was going to be a clear path. Everything at school was like it had been upon my prior return to school.

Everything, along with the positive vibes I felt in the air, made it seem like the tables would finally turn. Although none of the few classmates I once called my friend still showed no interest in resuming our friendship, it did not matter. I had what I could have wanted between the few friends I had outside of school and Trenton. Honestly, having any fake friends would have just been a problem. Nevertheless, after some time passed on our return to school and in the beginning years of our high school experience, it became apparent to me that nothing changed.

The same classmates who thought less of me had not changed their ways or their mindset of me being an outsider. Only, this time, it became much worse. Along with negative gossip going around again, I faced numerous vicious minor assaults. Some would be in the line of almost close to a simple touch, but others were just brutal. I would go to school every day with more fear than when I first became a victim of bullying.

Then, before I knew it, I found myself going back into the same hole I tried so hard to keep myself out. The teasing had gone completely unnoticed by any of my teachers. At the end of the day, though, they could only do so much, mainly because there were hundreds of students and only so many teachers. For the first time in my life, I felt utterly alone. The only ones I knew I could still trust were my entire family, Trenton, and the few personal close friends that I had both at home and at school. Even though I lived an extraordinary life at home, the fact that school became a living hell completely took a toll on my mental health.

The teasing took such a severe toll on me that my academic performance and attendance went down the drain. By the end of my first year of high school, I had missed twenty-six days of school. I cannot count how many of those days alone I completely lost my motivation to go to school. I woke up instantly with an emotional fear. I did not know the emotional torture waiting for me at school and decided to fake being sick.

On top of the absences from school, I failed in some classes to get the best grade possible. While in a few of my classes, I somehow managed to push myself enough to obtain an A or B. The teasing did enough damage that I ended other ones with a C or D. I will admit my classes were not the easiest due to my learning disability. Still, when you have gotten a completely broken mindset, it causes such a negative impact in your mind of everything put in front of you. I will never know that, if the bullying never took place, my grades would have been better. I do know, though, that my grades would have been better than what they were if the bullying never happened.

With me feeling completely lost and like I could barely trust anyone anymore, apart from my few loyal friends and family, I solely turned to the one gift that had never turned its back on me: music. As hard as it sounds, I always loved music. To me, it felt like it was the only aspect of life that was there when it seemed like to me that everything and everyone had disappeared. To me, the music lifted me in ways I thought was never possible. In a way, it made me feel whole again when I became completely broken and lost inside.

I could listen to any Linkin Park, Slipknot, or rock songs and feel like my life mattered again. Even to this day, how I managed to go from listening to a mixture of pop, rap, and a little country to rock music (notably Linkin Park) is a transition beyond explanation. I just knew the first time I heard "What I've Done" by Linkin Park on a TV commercial and listened to more of their songs, music forever changed my life. The light bulb I had been seeking since my negative return to school music had instantly flipped, and music had inhaled a purpose for my life into my body. The different themes of mental health represented in their music immediately felt like home to me. They resonated with me like anything else in my life.

So many people show negative feelings about Linkin Park's music because of the topics they address in the lyrics of the band's songs. For me, I could listen to those songs and feel at home and safe because of how much I resonated with those songs. Music was there for me whenever I needed it, especially when I needed somewhere to turn. Music became my sanctuary and my way of dealing with the emotional pain growing inside of me.

I could (and still can) listen to music and feel like my life matters in this cruel world. When I listened to music, everything negative around me went away. The second I heard a song by Linkin Park and other rock bands, happiness, and the security of knowing there is a significant reason for my existence prevailed. We all tend to deal with adversity in one or more forms of therapy, and my therapy became music.

While music did start helping me avoid going deeper into my dark hole, it could not change the mindset I began to develop toward the dark and cruel world that unfolded in front of me. To me, there was a world where I could trust and not feel vulnerable to showing who I indeed was. There now was a world I hated and betrayed me in more ways than I could have thought. As far as I knew, I could hardly trust nearly anybody anymore. The darkness from my situation at school started to fog my mind so badly that I found it hard to think straight.

Besides my family and a few friends, it felt like everyone else was out to get me. For the very first time in my life, I had reached absolute rock bottom. It impacted me more than I would have imagined. It showed me what nobody should ever have to experience. As much anger as I have ever felt in my life, nothing compared to the anger I was feeling.

As much anger was starting to build up inside of me, though, I never took it on the teachers or blamed them for what was happening. The teachers could only keep an eye on a student for so long, and when a teacher was not looking, that was the time a student picked on another helpless student. Everyone was doing their job in looking out for the children and giving them the best education possible. Nothing changed despite the help my teachers could give and the positive energy flowing from them that made some days at school more bearable.

Every attempt I took to try to ignore the hate at school or avoid being around those who took their frustrations out on me never worked. Some might ask why I did not decide to punch my bullies in the face, but I did not believe in violence. My parents instilled these principles in me from birth. Would I have taken that route now knowing what I know now? Yes, I would have. Much to my belief, the bullying did subside a little in my sophomore year and first semester of junior year, but it did not go entirely away.

As conflicted as I became, I knew I did not want to go on living feeling like a piece of trash and feeling helpless. Even today, I cannot remember in detail every suicide attempt I tried, but from what I remember, it was two or three. One that I somewhat remember is me sitting on my bed in my bedroom one day. It was one of those days I felt so alone and just wanted the emotional pain to end.

It felt like to me I was given so much more adversity and darkness in life that anyone should ever have to handle, and I did not want to go down that painful road anymore. I grabbed a grocery bag with no holes in it and put it over my head to suffocate myself but gave up after a few seconds. Deep down, I knew I could not go out that way. Even if the suicide attempts did work, it would only have passed my pain onto my loved ones.

Since I could not find a way to end the emotional despair through suicide, I turned to what nobody should ever have to endure, self-harm. As like the few suicide attempts, the full circumstances I cannot remember. It is particularly odd with the other dark traumatic events I mention that I can remember, but the full circumstances of my self-harm I cannot. What I can remember, though, is that whenever I felt a deep sense of despair after coming back home from school, I would go to my bedroom and cut myself. I had a pocket style knife, and I would basically rub it across my skin on one of my arms. The result was a scratch on my arm but not too deep, as if a cat scratched my arm. With the cuts not being too deep, it never left a permanent mark and completely healed after a few days. There was no doubt the cuts did not sting, but I needed a way to numb the emotional pain that I felt from the bullying at school. Music helped ease some of the emotional pain, but it only helped so much. The only option I could think of to numb the pain with the darkness I felt was self-harm.

Since I always did the self-harm in my bedroom with the door shut, and I cut myself on my lower part of my arm, my mother or nobody else around me never noticed the scratches on my arm. I wanted to tell my parents what was going on, but with the mental pain they both experienced in my cancer battles, I knew telling them would devastate them. So, I decided not to say anything. In my mind, I thought keeping the emotional pain away from my parents was the only choice. They already helped me get through my prior challenging battles, so I wanted to do it differently and win this battle myself.

The fact remained that I could not find the courage to tell one of my parents. My clouded mind only thought about the possible disappointment. I cannot count and do not want to think about how many days I spent conflicted on finally deciding to give up. As understanding I knew my parents would have been, all the possible adverse outcomes kept me at a standstill.

I experienced a different type of cry for help, but I only knew how to overcome a physical battle.

The one trait I tend to never forget, though, even in this period of my life, was the trait engraved in me through my past traumatic experiences, especially my experience at St. Jude. It took me so long to remember it again until I returned to Memphis in 2016 for my yearly St. Jude checkup. The trait of "hope and believe" given to me has always helped me through the previous worst times, even when I have become blind to it. While my appointment schedule was like my last checkups, my doctors decided to add an appointment with a licensed social worker over time. My doctors just felt how traumatic my transplant was, plus, adding in the previous trauma I went through before my cancer diagnosis, it was best to have that service.

Before I could look at the clock, I was back in Memphis, seeing the place I will always call a second home, St. Jude, for around five days. During my appointment with the social worker, she asked about how life was back home and how I liked school. For a very brief period, I finally decided to overcome my demons and tell the truth about my dark situation at school. I will admit that, as much as I wanted to keep on listening to my subconscious to keep on shoving the emotional pain down, I could not take the agony anymore. It was that I either confessed to the social worker or went back home to fully give in to my demons and finally end up perishing by my own hands.

She acted according to what her training teaches social workers, and the rest of the conversation went as usual. It felt like I had finally taken a tremendous weight off my shoulders, but I could not help the potential negative impact of hiding the truth. I went back home, not overthinking the situation. Then, my mother asked me about the reality of my life at school.

The social worker called her a few days after we got back from my checkup and told her what was truly going on with me at school. Deep down, I knew I could not hide the truth and confessed to my mother. The disbelief on her face was beyond hard on me, but she showed more understanding than anything else for my sake.

Without hesitation, she took me down to my school and confronted the principal. He was extremely saddened and furious to hear what was going on. After I told him about all my classmates who were bullying me, he brought them in individually to sign a contract. The contract said they could not be around me whenever it became avoidable. If any one of them attacked me either verbally or physically, the school would punish them. At around the same time, my mother also took me to the doctor so I could go on an antidepressant medication called Fluoxetine. It would keep my thoughts from getting any darker.

In addition to the changes, my school established a new procedure for me to report any further bullying incidents. Instead of reporting any problems to the principal, I would go to another school staff member, who would inform the principal of the status. They knew that going to that staff member instead of straight to the principal would not make it look like I ratted on my bullies. Despite the circumstances, I finally lifted the heavy weight of emotional despair off my shoulders.

However, the new battle of returning my mind to how it was and finding the will to continue attending school while being a snitch had begun. I became so lost in more ways than I could count, and not knowing if I would fully find myself scared me. I further felt conflicted about how I was not entirely myself. I lived under the outside shell of a lie inside my body. I was trying to make sense of how no one noticed or how my whole situation at school had gotten out of control, which added more fuel to the fire.

Following the changes and being under intense treatment for my mental health diagnosis, a fate I was looking forward to for too long came my way. All the physical attacks vanished, and only typical high school rumors remained. While I did experience a few very minor physical attacks, the daily taunting had been no more. I could not help but become happy that the ordeal had ended, but I still felt conflicted about my future. Not knowing whether I would find myself again left a tremendous number of painful mental scars.

A few weeks after going on antidepressants, I met with the school's guidance counselor to do my class schedule for the fall semester. Somehow, even with the one class I failed, I gained enough credits to be eligible for early graduation. All that remained was taking the remaining required classes and a few electives. If I chose to graduate one semester early, I would have to choose between two options: either receive my diploma in December or walk in the traditional ceremony in May of next year and receive my diploma then. Whatever I decided, my high school journey would end in December. It was just a matter of whether I wanted to walk in the official graduation ceremony.

There is no doubt that at first I struggled with the thought, but after reverting to my entire high school living hell ordeal, I quickly decided to say yes to graduating early. The one decision I felt even more conflicted about was taking part in the graduation ceremony. I wanted to walk with my small handful of classmates who were there for me until the end, including Trenton. Nevertheless, I could not get over the thought of being near the ones who did nothing but make my high school experience a living hell.

I returned home from school that same day and told my mother I said yes to graduating early. I further explained my original idea of skipping the ceremony. Her instant reply was, "Well, if you don't want to walk, there is no need for a graduation party." After several hours of carefully thinking about its significant accomplishment, I changed my mind. With me being my mom's first child with a high school diploma, I knew how much it meant to her to see me walk across the stage.

Trauma and my demons robbed me of many chances, and I simply could not let trauma rob me of this chance. My father supported my decision but did not agree to miss a semester of more memories. There will always be a small part of me that wishes I did go an extra semester, but the severe damage to my mental health already happened. As much as I would have liked, I could not rewrite the past, and it simply became time to take back my life.

I returned to the school counselor the next day and said yes to walking in the ceremony. I took the final leap to take an enormous weight off my shoulders and could not be happier. My last semester went by slowly, but most of it was due to me not skipping as much. The whole bullying situation at school died down, and for the first time, I got on the straight path to getting all A's and B's. I will admit I did think back to my decision, but I knew the damage from all the previous years could not be irreversible. The place I once loved remained a dead ruin to me, and a successful semester could not change that.

Despite finally reaching the finish line and walking across the stage to receive my diploma, I could not help but think about the uncertainty of my college situation. I became so excited at the new opportunity but was still beyond terrified about the unknown. I struggled so badly through my middle and high school years, and the trauma left me with more anxiety than ever in my life. The whole dreadful experience left me with more than damaging scars. It left me with a lack of permanent social skills, and my turn to escape reality only ended up adding to it.

I went to bed every night thinking, "What if my college experience is going to be just like my school experience was upon my return from my second battle with cancer?" I knew, though, that once I met with my advisor at Black Hawk College and registered for classes, I would have to rely solely on fate. Even after BHC, would my transfer to Western Illinois University be what I sought in my high school experience?

# 11

# Ray of Light

If there existed a time in my life filled with more anxiety than I could count, it would be the few weeks before my first day of college. I was so excited to start a new chapter in my life, but I still felt conflicted because of the adversity I went through on my return to school. For all that I knew, it would just be a fifty-fifty chance. Either college would be a do-over of high school, or it would be the ray of light I had been looking for all along.

Now, I also had finally overcome a different life battle in surviving my near-fatal depression and stopped myself from further turning to self-harm. I knew there was another severe problem that I needed to fix. I needed to find the person I once became following the conclusion of my first cancer battle. I needed to dig up the true Jacob slowly buried through enduring all the trauma he did. I was wearing a false mask to hide the agony tearing me up. My subconscious convinced me that keeping the pain from my loved ones was the right decision.

I became beyond lost inside of my skin. I ran away from the truth soon as my long-lasting battle with normalcy seemed unbeatable, but I could not run away anymore. On top of that problem, I had to figure out the trust issues I let build inside of my skin through my high school years. I once trusted so many at school, especially the few I used to call friends. For them to turn on me left an emotional scar more impactful than anything else in my life.

Before I knew it, the day of meeting my fate and unknown judgment came as I woke up to get in my car and drive to campus for my first day of college. The inside of me had nothing but fear and anxiety, but the moment I walked through the front lobby's doors, it was fight or flight. The first class of my college experience ended up going nowhere in terms of making a massive turnaround in my life. I walked in to feel the positive vibe from the room and the instructor. However, I became numb. I was barely able to get words to come out of my mouth, and just sat down to get through the class period.

I headed to my next class with the same emotions as my prior class. This time, though, a particular aspect changed. I walked inside the classroom to look at the open seat options but noticed only a few available. At first, I could not decide where to sit, but I saw a fellow student, Jade, pointing out an open seat by her. As scared as I wanted to be, I decided to outweigh my subconscious and took a leap of faith. She introduced herself before the start of class, and after catching my breath, I told her about me.

I managed to push through what will always be my most significant barrier through reaching out and opening to Jade in class. Much to my expectations, it did not backfire on me. After class ended, we learned of a few similar courses in our schedules. We learned more about each other, which led me to change my perspective of being willing to open to others. Even with me leaving somewhat of a guard up, I built enough courage to talk to some of the others in my other classes. I took a chance I thought would never happen, and the unbelievable came out.

I learned that we were all trying to figure out this new part of our lives at the end of the day. Whether I wanted to believe it, we all were human beings just trying to find our place in the latest chapter in our lives. Cancer or a mental illness might not have affected the individuals around me, but there was no doubt they all had faced their own obstacles in life. While some around me may not have been thrilled about co-existing with me, they did show traits of understanding and compassion for me, different from what I never received from some of my classmates in high school. The matter, too, was that I honestly did not want to be a part of the popular crowd in college. I still wanted to be a part of a group I could call my friends and where I belonged, which is what I got in college.

Once I managed to push past breaking outside my shell unexpectedly, I wanted to take another chance by signing up for a few different student organizations. Being involved in soccer back in elementary school gave me an indescribable feeling, and I wanted to get that feeling back. Without much hesitation and once again overcoming initial fear, I decided to take a chance at the Math & Science Club and Circle K. The Circle K service-based club was a newbie student organization. Still, after seeing the impactful work of St. Jude, I decided to take a chance on that student organization, which was understandable to others.

My second semester went further uphill and only got better. I learned a unique perspective on life through my positive college experience while continuing to build unforgettable memories. The perspective is that, while there will always be a dark piece in the world, there will always be a light at the other end of the spectrum. I also strengthened my knowledge through college classes and met more unfamiliar faces.

I met one face, Koda, in my Math Literacy class. We instantly could relate to our ongoing college experience, becoming good friends in no time. Like Jade, we had a few similar courses. So, we often went to the student cafeteria to talk and work on whatever college homework we had. Plus, he eventually met Jade after some time, so we all became good friends in a few weeks.

To put it simply, within my first year of college, my whole life changed. For the first time in a long time, my life started to go in the direction I wanted it to for so long. It became everything for which I hoped. Best of all, nobody taunted me for being who I was. I finally found the person that was lost in the darkness for so long. I knew there was always going to be a piece of me that I would not ever recover due to the turmoil of my past trauma, but that did not mean college could not be a fresh start to find a new path in life and re-discover myself.

The rest of my journey at Black Hawk College was as unique as possible. I met more classmates to whom I could relate and became further involved on campus. I took a chance on more than I initially thought of during my time there. Particularly, my willingness to open myself to others left me with an experience more meaningful than anything else. I had seen how I was wrong in my new philosophy of the world due to my rough, severe mental illness encounter. There was no doubt a part of me that would remain on guard upon my start at Western, but at least now I had developed a sense of who I could trust. I wish that guard could go away, but I committed myself to not returning to the dark, empty void I in which I had once found myself laid captive.

The first major decision I had to consider before I started my first semester at Western Illinois University was whether I wanted to live on or off campus. At that time, I was still living in the same town, around an hour and a half from campus. While WIU required first-year college students to live on campus, once a student had sixty or more credits, WIU removed the requirement. I could have enjoyed saving money and living at home, but a three-hour drive five times a week would be outrageous.

I knew the day I got my acceptance letter from WIU that I wanted to make the most out of my journey at WIU (and the last two years of college). I knew I still wanted to work some, so I had at least a little money available, but not the number of hours I had worked while attending BHC. Given that neither my mother's nor father's income would be enough to support my part of the monthly apartment rent with the inefficient income, I knew there was only one choice. The choice was to take another chance and sign up to live on campus.

Luckily, during my second WIU campus visit, I saw an unoccupied room in Thompson Hall. Call it fate, but I knew the day I committed to living on campus that I wanted Thompson Hall to be a part of my WIU experience. Thompson Hall had all the exact amenities I needed and was within walking distance of where my classes was located. While one current WIU student did give me a tour of Corbin-Olson during my first WIU visit, Thompson stood out to me more.

Thompson Hall also offered a transfer year experience community. The program was for all the interested incoming transfer students, which allowed them to live on the same floor together. The main goal of the experience was for all the transfer students to find a connection with one another through their college experience. Once I had taken in all the facts, I knew with all my heart that I needed to put the transfer floor in Thompson Hall on my WIU housing application. The only other task I would need to do was find a roommate through WIU's roommate matching system.

As with any other college enrollment, a day also came for the incoming student to officially register for their college classes. As with other universities, WIU had a separate orientation program for new students and those with some college experience. It was not a system to make all of us seem different. It was just a way for the transfer students to avoid committing more time to learn about the various college resources (financial aid, on-campus housing, etc.) during our orientation, which we already knew. While I could have registered in the summer after graduating from Black Hawk, I decided to choose a day to register in April, about a month before I graduated.

Having almost two years of college, I had two options. I could have gone to campus and met with my advisor to register for classes or attended a transfer new student orientation program. It did not take long to decide to participate in the transfer new student orientation program. Especially counting the hour-and-a-half drive to campus for me, why not make the drive worth it?

Weeks later, I arrived on campus early on a Friday morning and parked by the University Union, where WIU held most of the orientation sessions. Even though I tried to encourage myself to talk to new people, I found myself unable to get any words to come out when I did walk into the building (well, except for the WIU staff member checking us in). The situation was unfortunate, but I decided not to let the negative get the best of me and continue through the three-hour orientation.

While I could not find the inner strength to talk to some of my fellow incoming WIU students, there was one familiar fellow transfer student. Ryan was a fellow incoming transfer student majoring in the same broadcasting emphasis as me but with different minors. Before registration day, we encountered each other's profiles on Western's roommate matching system. Unfortunately for me, Ryan had already found a roommate, but we decided to introduce ourselves online. When I attended the orientation course registration session, we recognized each other and said hello. Although WIU decided to do most of the orientation sessions with everyone as a whole group, the prospective students went to groups that their major was in for the registration part. We talked for however long we could before we all sat in front of a computer to sign onto Student/Alumni Records System (STARS) - Western's system - to register for the classes. These had been decided in advance by our advisor. We talked a bit more on our way out of the building after officially registering for classes.

Even before officially starting my WIU journey, I knew our friendship would be great. On top of our having the same broadcasting major emphasis, we discovered some similarities. We both listened to rock music and were massive Linkin Park fans. He also shared some negative adversity in life due to being different. As expected, we both ended up with similar classes in our schedules. So, I could not be happier to strengthen our bond further.

Despite being beyond excited and ready for the next chapter at WIU, I did not want to leave behind the journey I started at BHC. I met many amazing people and made many great memories, and for the train to stop rolling sent a shockwave through my body. From my first day of college, I knew my time would go by quickly. Sadly, we often do not take the time to realize how fast time indeed passes by, and I had not taken the time to think about it until I walked across the stage to receive my diploma cover at my BHC graduation. For me, overcoming those complex barriers caused by earlier trauma, along with pushing through the typical challenges for college students, made my graduation an even more unique achievement.

Although I reached a significant milestone in my life, I could not stop thinking about my next stop at WIU. Deep in my heart, I knew my experience there would be great, like my BHC one. However, with me being a reasonable distance away from home since I decided to live on campus, it would be a different challenge. I had many of my close friends and family members close to me in my times of great despair, especially in my cancer battles. This time, though, I would have to learn to adapt without being in the direct presence of my loved ones.

There is no doubt they would be a phone call away, but it was evident that I had to start finding a way to build my inner strength and fully take back the person I once was. My experience at BHC allowed me to rediscover myself while finally discovering the light from the darkness that had once plagued my childhood. I knew it would also become time to finish that self-rediscovery journey at WIU. Moreover, I could only do that by learning how to take back my life once laid captive by trauma. I was beyond frightened to take on this task, yet I strongly knew it was time to finish taking back my sense of pride and the life I knew.

After one summer of my last shifts ever at a McDonald's restaurant near where I was living and two classes to fully finish the requirements of my associate degree, my transfer to WIU was around the corner. Since I could not find any close friends going to WIU, I fully committed to finding a roommate through Western's roommate matching system. As bad as I would have liked a single dorm room, the price for one was too much for my financial situation. After searching on WIU's system STARS, I found Weston's page on my matches.

We both had the same dorm and similar answers to living

preferences. I requested Weston to be my roommate and let fate decide the rest. After several days, he saw it and accepted it. In the following days, we messaged each other via the system to get to know each other. Then, we moved to Snapchat. As expected, we did have some differences, but we did hit it off, especially since we both were broadcasting majors but with different emphases.

I had already spent several days trying to figure out what to bring to campus besides the apparent essentials and what to fit all my stuff in. Luckily, Trenton had dorm life experience under his belt, so I asked him for his advice. He suggested using duffel bags, so I went to a Walmart near where I was living and bought two duffel bags. I fit a good pile of clothes and everything for my bedding into both bags and a carry-on suitcase while fitting everything else in the few bags I already had.

I shoved most of what I packed into my Chevy Impala and the rest of it into my mom's Trailblazer. I returned home that late afternoon from a quick run to a surprise. Trenton came over to let me know he planned to help me move into my dorm, along with my mother and one of my sisters. As much as I hate mornings, I managed to get my body up around seven a.m. to hit the road because the suggested arrival time was nine a.m. Trenton rode with me so he could park my car once we arrived on campus. My sister and mother followed us in my mom's Trailblazer.

We arrived at campus after a long ride there, but in realtime, it was only close to an hour and a half. As soon as we came near Thompson Hall, officers of the Western's Office of Public Safety directed every person to the unloading area, followed by the parking area. The entire area in front of the dorm was a circus of both students and family or friends. Some were waiting with their belongings for a cart, some were unloading, and others were walking into check-in. To make the move into our dorm as easy as possible, all of us students checked in, grabbed both our keys (while someone stayed with our belongings), and then waited for a cart for someone from the volunteer Western welcome crew to become available. After a short wait, my turn for a cart came. Somehow, I managed to fit everything except for my backpack and a small bag in it. Everyone with me and I headed up and walked into my dorm room. The room was not as the cinema shows it, but it was still all that I imagined it to be. Not long after we got into the room and I started to unpack some of my belongings, my resident assistant, Leo, stopped by to introduce himself to us. I noticed he was (and still is!) a great guy, and I was excited to get to know him.

My roommate, Weston, had a later move-in time, so I decided to at least get my bedding set on my twin-size bed. I further got whatever I could unpacked. We had decided to go ahead and grab lunch while I waited for Weston to arrive with his belongings. Since Weston and I communicated through Snapchat in the weeks before move-in day, we had already developed a solid plan for our room layout. I did not end up eating at any of the local restaurants during my previous two campus visits. Because of this, I was not surprised to see all the popular ones in town packed. After looking around town for a while, we found a Mexican restaurant, and the food was surprisingly good.

By the time I returned to campus, Weston arrived not too long after we left and got his belongings moved into our room. He also had left campus to grab lunch with his family, so we decided to sit outside and spend more time together until he returned. To my surprise, time played in both our flavors. Weston was wrapping up lunch not exceptionally long upon my return to campus. I do not want to think about how much

I unnecessarily flooded his Snapchat, but it was just because of how excited I was to meet him.

Since my mother, sister, and Trenton expressed exhaustion from the move-in, they decided to head back home once Weston and his parents returned to campus, which happened quickly. They did not take long to return to campus and walk up to us. Weston and I did not waste time shaking hands and letting everyone else introduce themselves. I could not have been happier to meet Weston and his awesome parents in person.

Before I could count, it became time to say goodbye, or as I like to call it, "see you later," to my two family members and Trenton. We all shed a little tear upon saying those words, but we also deeply knew it was not indeed goodbye. All were simply a phone call away. Weston's parents went back up to our room to help us finish setting up and we did not mind the extra help. Despite how exhausted I had already become; I could not have been happier with the final setup of our room. It was not close to my dream home or a fancy apartment/house, but it was a room I knew I would enjoy spending time in.

Luckily, most transfer residents on the floor had moved into their rooms by that point. So, Weston and I decided to start getting acquainted with some of our floormates before the move-in weekend activities began. Since we all were stuck with each other for the school year, why not start developing new friendships? During the rest of that afternoon, we met Drake, Mike, Brock, Jaxon, Sam, Steve, Lucian, Theo, Zane, Nathan, Teagan, and Joel.

What came as a great surprise was seeing Dante and Jack again. We first became acquainted through our time at BHC. Jack was a member of the Science & Math Club for a while after I joined, and I first saw Dante through one of my upper-level

English classes. I got to know both throughout those situations, but since we did not get to know each other personally, neither learned of our decision to transfer to WIU.

Another memory I will always treasure is all the welcome weekend activities WIU held for all the new students. Events included a welcome picnic behind the union, the annual university assembly, Rocky After Dark, and other events. Before the start of Rocky After Dark, though, every floor had to have a mandatory meeting for the RA to review the small handful of rules and let all the residents introduce themselves. The first day alone kept me so busy that I was surprised I managed to squeeze some free time in that Friday to pick up the mini fridge my father and former stepmother bought me.

I knew from my involvement in on-campus student organizations at BHC, which turned out successful, that I wanted to continue at WIU. So, I did not hesitate to attend the activities fair with a few of my floormates, which took place during the first week of the school semester. I had already become aware of the student-run radio station, 88.3 The Dog, through my previous campus tour, but I still wanted to see what other opportunities there were. We headed to the fair, and I could not believe all the different organizations.

I found some additional appealing organizations from my research before my transfer: RockyThon (Formerly Dance Marathon) and Western Technical Services (WESTEC). One of my dad's military friends went to WIU in the past and worked for WESTEC. So, he encouraged me to work for them. He knew my interest in sound and emphasized how working for them would help build my résumé. After I thought deeply about it, I knew working for them and being a DJ with 88.3 The Dog would give me some unforgettable memories and experiences to reflect on after graduation.

RockyThon is another organization I quickly glanced at in my prior research but only thought a little of it due to the name. Despite only a few other organizations not standing out to me, fate or something unexplainable told me to take a second look at the RockyThon table. At first, I thought, "Well, I'm not into dancing," but once I stopped and learned of the organization's purpose, I instantly became hooked. I learned RockyThon raises money for crucially ill children at the St. Louis Children's Miracle Network Hospital, including children with cancer. I knew what I had to participate and agreed to get involved. Due to the WESTEC staff being at its maximum capacity, I could not get in quite yet. However, the current WESTEC president kept my information on file for a potential future interview.

By the end of the weekend, we also found another way to get closer and develop our floor bond through an idea from Leo. During the weekdays (and whenever possible on the weekends), we all met by the elevator around the same time to go down to the dining hall and eat dinner together. Leo frequently joined us. There were so many of us that we pushed at least a few tables together, but the conversations will always be priceless! The bond increased, and we found activities to do together, either on or off campus.

Beyond the new perspective I was obtaining living in Thompson, I started to make unforgettable memories in both my classes and as a broadcasting student. One came several days into the semester when I arrived early to one of my upper-level classes. To pass some time while I waited for the class instructor to arrive, I decided to sit on a small couch outside of the classroom and noodle around on my phone. Not too long after I sat, a senior broadcast student I saw during my previous second campus visit arrived to wait for class. Since the instructor was not there yet, he decided to sit on the other side of the couch and talk to me after recognizing me.

He asked how my WIU experience was shaping out, how my classes were going, and whatnot. Not long after he arrived, one of his friends (also a senior), whom I also saw during my second visit, came, and talked to us right after he recognized me. I would eventually speak to both here and there during the semester when we saw each other on the broadcasting floor and in class. For them to show they fully acknowledged my presence and that they cared about me meant a lot to me. They showed that, in a challenging time, my life did matter after trauma. Some of my elementary and high school classmates had taken that away in my prior return to elementary school, and it is an experience I will always treasure.

While I did miss home, I wanted to take advantage of the free time I got on the weekends (particularly Fridays and Saturdays) to remain on campus. On the weekends, I did not return home. I attended a campus event or found an activity to do with a few of my floormates or Ryan. Unexpectedly, I even went out with several of my floormates to experience the night drinking life in Macomb. Although I did not join them during the first weekend of the semester due to returning home, I decided to retake a chance on fate.

I will admit that despite feeling weird at first because I never experienced it before, I realized the main benefit of going out. I have never been big on drinking, but what I always enjoy is creating life-lasting, unforgettable memories. Going out with floormates was one way to do that. Luckily, that sudden positive mindset paid off on one specific weekend. We often went to the Forum, a familiar spot for the party life in town. One night out, we met a fellow WIU student, Jessica, and her friend Skylynn. As we all got to know each other, Jessica and Skylynn became part of the group my friends and I formed. I could not have been happier with the unique experience.

In a matter of weeks into my first semester, my entire experience at Western shaped into the miracle I needed. All of us living on the floor became more than floormates. Even though everyone came from diverse backgrounds, we all were humans. In a flash, I had amazing friends who cared deeply about me. Nobody judged me for who I was. Best of all, I realized my entire college experience was more than just getting a valuable education. It was a time for me to build a fresh start and genuinely see that I was not the pile of trash my trauma convinced me I was.

In my second semester and moving forward, it only became a better, fantastic college experience. I became involved further on campus by getting a job through WESTEC (after some staff openings came up) and joining the National Broadcasting Association student club. I also joined the student-run newscast, News3, after a classmate currently involved in both student organizations had encouraged me. The bond between most of us on the floor grew strong enough that, through some help from Leo, we decided to make a group move for the next school year. We were going to be able to remain together while still having Leo as our resident assistant. I could not think of anything better.

Just as my move into my college dorm in my first year at WIU came with meeting new fellow college students, the move in for my second year at WIU came with additional fresh faces. Despite our group not finding a bond between us and them, there was one person with whom we found a connection later in the school year. Marc started his journey at WIU in January of 2021 (also being my final semester of college). He moved into the same floor in a room close to Weston and me. As fate magically had it, he was a transfer student like us, simply trying to make the best of his college experience.

Marc was extremely outgoing, and it did not take long for my WIU friends to see that. They decided to go ahead and get to know more about him and asked Marc to join them at the Forum one weekend. Something came up for me, so I did not join them that night. At first, I debated whether I should have become acquainted with him due to the limited time left in the semester (about fourteen weeks) until the end of my WIU journey as a student.

At that point, it also did not help that a small part of me would still always remain on guard of attachments I make due to my past trauma. It changed, though, after I finally convinced myself, he deserved (like others) a chance. My trauma taught me so much, and it certainly taught me that, despite there being people with bad intentions in the world, there will always be good people. In the following days, I learned more about Marc, and I did not regret the decision. He is a great and caring person, and it did not take long for me to see that.

When I started college, I thought of getting almost nothing, but the truth is, I ended up with more than I pictured. Ever since my first traumatic encounter with Macrocephaly with Ventriculomegaly, I wanted a ray of light to tell me I was not the worthless person my trauma made me out to be. Through my triumph, I finally found my answer through my college experience. I witnessed the wrath of the darkness in life and thought of nothing but the bad in the world, but my entire college journey proved me wrong.

It taught me a key fact: in some corners, there is going to be bad, but that does not mean it has to make you blind to all the good that does exist in the world. I witnessed the greatest wrath of the darkness in elementary and high school, but much to my initial belief, the light finally prevailed. When I walked across the stage at my WIU graduation ceremony, I knew I would be walking away with way more than an education, and that is what I received through my college experience. To walk away with not just a bachelor's degree in broadcast production but to overcome my most significant barrier through my college journey will always be my greatest victory.

# 12

# Tattoo
# (Interlude, part 2)

If there is one happy memory that I will never be able to forget in life, it is when I said yes to receiving my very first tattoo. I become interested in tattoos during my teenage years. I could not precisely ever tell myself what exact aspect of a tattoo drew me in, but I became drawn to the art aspect of a tattoo. Ever since my first encounter with the song "What I've Done" by Linkin Park and the life-changing experience with the film *Spectacular*, I have viewed the aspect of art/storytelling in all mediums the same, and how similar they all are to each other.

When I turned sixteen, I made it my mission to persuade my mother to permit me to get my first tattoo. With nothing else coming to my mind, I went to my mother and said, "I either want both of my ears pierced or a tattoo." Unexpectedly, my mother still stood against the thought of something like ink going into my skin due to my two childhood cancer battles. Nevertheless, she said yes to getting both of my ears pierced because earrings are not as severe as tattoo ink.

Fast forward several months later to a day I can never forget. Both of my sisters were over at the house (the same one we had moved to after my first cancer battle) and talked to my mother as usual. They said they booked an appointment to get matching sister tattoos. Unexpectedly, my mother asked me if I wanted to get my first tattoo through the same artist.

At first, I was speechless, but I quickly turned that shocked feeling into excitement. The main (but minor) barrier I had to figure out was what I should get. Although it took several minutes and looking at my mother's St. Jude tattoo, I realized the best choice was the St. Jude logo, but with "survivor" underneath it. It was only because of the significant impact St. Jude has had on my life, while also to celebrate me overcoming all odds in my cancer battles.

The next day, my sisters, a few other family members, and I went to get our new tattoos. The artist we went with did not have his own studio, so we met up with others at the house of one of my sister's boyfriend's (now brother-in-law) close friends. Everyone thought I was going to be scared once the needle went into my skin, but I was not. It was due to when nurses had to insert a long needle into my skin during my cancer treatment.

After what felt like an entire day, the tattoo was complete after about an hour. I could not have been happier with the final picture. Intentionally, I did not plan to have the year "2009" in the tattoo. When the artist asked me if there was anything I wanted to put in the free space between the bottom of the St. Jude logo and the top of Survivor, I replied, "2009." It will always be a significant year to me since it is the year that I was reborn with a greater purpose in life, so I knew it needed to be a part of the tattoo.

To anybody, my first tattoo can emphasize the celebration

of me being another miracle cancer survivor. To me, though, the tattoo will always be more than me overcoming cancer twice. It will always symbolize the great triumph I achieved from everything the darkness handed down to me from birth. The tattoo will always represent the unique survivor that God has instilled in me through my challenging trials from both childhood and adolescent trauma.

# 13

## Questionable Doubt

If there is one truth that came from beating cancer, it is that it is never truly over. I thought to myself that when I recovered from my bone marrow transplant, my battle with cancer came to a complete close. After I completed the year of an abnormal lifestyle to recover fully from my transplant, I thought I would be set entirely free from the withhold of the cancer. I soaked in the truth of all the terrible side effects that came with winning my battle with cancer while learning to cope with the sudden changes in my life. What I did find hard to face for so long was the fear that now would be with me for the rest of my life.

As cancer survivors, we often think we become invisible to further problems associated with either our previous cancer treatments or the cancer itself. Whether it be a potential future cancer relapse, potential future fatal complications related to our prior cancer treatment, or even the diagnosis of a different type of cancer. I cannot speak for every cancer survivor, but I believed that the horror would finally be over following the triumph of my second cancer battle. With all my heart, I wanted to be true that life gave me the chance to live the rest of whatever time fate had stored in me peacefully, but it is the opposite.

The truth was that the finish line was only the beginning of the fact that, even though I survived both of my cancer battles, it did not make me completely invisible from cancer. I cannot tell you how many times I have read of many cancer survivors overcoming their struggle to end up having fate take them due to their cancer returning or due to medical complications associated with their previous cancer treatment. Some survivors even perished due to the diagnosis of a different type of cancer. It ended up taking much longer than it should have, but I slowly accepted the realization that, despite surviving my cancer, it was not entirely over. My bone marrow transplant gave me the security of knowing my cancer should not return. However, it still cannot block any potentially deadly side effects or the possible diagnosis of a different type of cancer.

One of my science professors back at BHC told the classroom in a lecture that cancer is not just one disease; it is many diseases. In a tiny way, I was in some denial for so long that my war with cancer was not entirely over, but I knew from that day on that I had to accept the change. While I did claim victory in beating my non-Hodgkin's Lymphoma, my bone marrow transplant was a cure for that type of cancer. However, it was not a cure for a different type of cancer with any future rough side effects. I wanted to think cancer would be a part of the past, but when I experienced my cancer relapse, it changed that exact thought forever. The very day the doctors informed me my cancer was back, I knew the truth that, in a way, I would only be safe from non-Hodgkin's Lymphoma.

Although this fear will remain with me for the rest of my life, I know I should not let it consume me at the same time and define whatever life I have left. Without a doubt, I will continue to live each day to the fullest potential and make the life St. Jude gave me as magnificent as possible. Cancer took some of my security, but it did not take away the gift of living the best life I can. However, I certainly will not lie about never knowing the answer to the question, "Is my battle with cancer over?" It will always be the worst cancer side effect I will ever know.

# 14

## What Did Keep Me Alive

Reverting at everything I have gone through has given me more uncertainty than ever, mainly because of the answers behind my triumph I never received (and will never know). I have always traveled through a lengthy search in my mind to answer why I did not perish a long time ago, if not by cancer, by my own hands from the great wrath of depression. In no way is this not letting my demons speak for me, but rather the truth of considering all the adversity I have endured throughout my life in both my childhood and adolescent years. I survived so much more than any single individual shall have to experience, taking in not only my cancer and mental health battle but every dreadful diagnosis handed to me after birth.

Every day I wake up, and life reminds me of the survival skills I did manage to pick up and carry into battle throughout my experience. However, I also cannot look past all the dark times when I wanted to bow down to the darkness and fully give up. I wanted to give in more times than I can count, especially after I reached my breaking point in life after returning to school from my bone marrow transplant. Despite never knowing the true answer, I have always wondered, in my sense of thought, what got me through all the trauma handed down to me.

Was it the hope I ended up finding in the darkest situations? Was it my determination to see my triumph despite the adversity life threw at me? Was it the light at the end of an unforeseen tunnel that came out of me from turning to music in my darkest times? Was it my beloved family and friends who were always there for me, even when the darkness told me differently? Was it God being there for me all along, despite me turning my back on him several times? Was it the strength I learned how to carry with me throughout my entire traumatic experience? Was it just simply the sincere hope and the fighter God predestined in me at birth to which I had become blind to all along?

Even though I will never know the exact reason, I know it was a combination of all the questions above. Music was there to keep me from completely drowning in the darkness, but looking back, music was not the only aspect that kept me alive. The truth is that countless lights have always supported me afloat through it all. My family and faithful friends, hope I first engraved through my experience at St. Jude, and God's will and strength handed down to me at birth, and music brought me through it. Most importantly, it was my determination to see my profound triumph. They all have always played an equal role in my existence today. In a significant way, music gave me the inner voice I was looking for and motivation to keep pushing forward, but so did all the other gifts trauma give to me over time.

# 15

## Final Closure and Moving Forward

If there is one painful aspect of going through traumatic experiences, it is genuinely accepting what is now out of your reach while finding the faith to move forward in a positive light. Trauma changes our perspective on both life and the world. I honestly know I do not have to say proven facts to back that statement. We all are humans given the same characteristic at birth, which is the ability to feel pain. Everybody is born into this world with a different path in life.

I have always thought at the very beginning of my healing process of how different my life could have been if I lived a normal life at birth. What if life had never diagnosed me with macrocephaly with ventriculomegaly? What if life had never diagnosed me with a developmental delay? What if life had never diagnosed me with a speech disability? What if my parents had never separated? What if a cancer diagnosis never came into my life, or if cancer ended its attempt after my battle? What if my return to school had not been so brutal? What if I had never fallen victim to depression? What if my life had just been normal from the start?

I will not lie and say these questions did not bother me when I began my healing process after my high school graduation. I know life cannot be perfect, and, as I have said before, whether we like it or not, we will go through life's challenges. To me, though, it just seemed like a huge burden to go through so many experiences. I have always been a fighter like many from birth, but to have to tackle one dreadful experience after another became too much. I had finally given in to the darkness and turned to the only aspect of life I came to know depression and, worst of all, true hopelessness.

What I now know by looking back at it with a new perspective is that my healing has given me everything, and life happens for a reason. I have always hated the fact that life has given me so much despair and not enough positivity to balance it out, but I know it was not for nothing. We are all given a different path from birth, and any adversity is to shape our purpose in life, handed by God. Always remember that life's challenges are not to bring you any harm but to guide you to your specific path. Everybody goes through different obstacles in life, but that is simply what makes each one of us unique in our way and makes us human.

While I did not want to believe it, whether I liked it or not, I did bring a good amount of harm to myself in the time of my suffering that I could have easily avoided. I was bittersweet towards the world, God, and specific individuals for all the darkness that has plagued my life. For so long, I did not want to face the fact that I caused an enormous weight on my shoulders by holding onto the anger. Though I know now, through my healing, that I had to accept my role to move forward positively. What I did to myself is in the past now, and I know I should not let it stop me from continuing in life.

I made the decision back then to keep my mental illness in the dark from several of my friends and family members, but I know it was a wrong decision to make. Back then, I thought with the unrealistic mindset I developed, that hiding the weight of the pain tearing me inside was a viable choice. I thought my family and everyone else around me had already suffered enough through my horrible cancer experience. So, why should I put this additional burden on them?

I thought I had made the right choice, but now thinking about the further negative consequences, it was not the choice I should have made. Despite it being hard to tell our loved ones what is really going on, battling a severe illness alone is harder. While we may think hiding any pain from the ones around us who genuinely care about it is better, the potential negative consequences that can arise from it are not worth it. When I looked back at that moment, letting them in might have led me to keep myself from drowning in as much pain as I did.

However, the one pill that has always seemed hard to grasp is forgiving every single person who has caused me pain, especially my bullies, from birth to the first day I started my treatment for depression. The thought of forgiving those who have done nothing but made my life more miserable left me conflicted, even when I became clean from self-harm after being on antidepressants. I thought, why should I forgive those who pushed me to the ground instead of lifting me? Then, one day, I saw a picture of a quote on social media that completely changed my perspective.

It briefly mentioned forgiving those who did you wrong because your healing is more important than you continuing to suffer on the inside of you. At first, I resisted the thought, but I was wrong after thinking about how I could not continue my healing path by holding on to the smoke. I needed to forgive those who did me wrong for my stake and peace. I needed to make the hard decision to live the rest of whatever life I have gotten without anger and embark on a new path of peace.

Forgiving is never forgetting about what happened in the past, so never disregard that. If anyone who did me wrong in life is reading this, I fully forgive you and hope for the best in your future. I could have kept holding onto the smoke I caused to myself in the past, but I know very well it is time for me to forgive myself of those burdens fully. Life is too short for the negative to hold you down, so I cannot let my role in my suffering keep me from pushing onward. If you can even have one key takeaway from my own experience, it is to forgive yourself for all the circumstances that have happened and will happen in your life that are beyond your control.

I wish I could go back and fully recover the exact Jacob that once existed after my first cancer battle, but that is a mission that has always been impossible to achieve. Whether I like it or not, a small piece of him perished a long time ago. When I finally rose from the ashes of my depression and re-discovered myself, a new person was born. A person with a different mindset and a unique perspective on everything.

I will always remain the same on the outside, but the inside of me will always remain changed by the truth my trauma gave me. The Jacob that all my loved ones knew from birth will always exist because I know I cannot forget what I stood for in this life from birth. Only, I will not ever be able to see the world the same way due to the childhood and adolescent trauma I experienced. It will forever be with me, but it serves as a great reminder of the hell I endured and what I do not want for my future. Trauma kept me hostage through darkness for too long, but it is now time for me to push forward.

If there is a bigger truth I quickly found, it is that complete healing takes time. While most of my wounds have healed throughout my healing process, there will always be some that will take more time. My survivor's guilt, some of the sorrow I could have easily avoided, and little reminders of the past will always take more time than I realized. By now, I know that I cannot be a stranger to the fact that some wounds take more time to heal, and it is not my fault. It is just how the healing process works.

What I have managed to find to keep me afloat through the rest of my wounds healing is the new light for which I was previously hunting. When I finally accepted help and cleared my mind, I realized the light that shone from my triumph. This new light will always remind me that my story is not over. I certainly have much more to live for than that. If I do know one straight fact, pain, in the end, is not supposed to be a means to an end but a guide to an unexpected path. To anyone who needs to hear this: whatever you are going through, you will get through it; I believe in you.

It is so easy for anyone who has become a victim of any form of childhood or adolescent trauma to end up thinking that their life meant nothing. All life has given them is a pile of rocks and a cloud of darkness with no hope. I once thought I was the darkness that plagued my childhood and adolescence. I used to think that I was merely alive to be a punching bag to life itself.

It took me several days of taking my antidepressants to real-ize for myself I, all along, was the light in my story and never the darkness. The darkness may have thought it had a grip on me through my trauma, but I had found my destiny in my life by being the light all along, even when I became blind to it. I know with all my heart that I am not the only one out there, as every survivor of any form of trauma is that light in their own story.

It will always be challenging, but one important lesson I have learned you can take forward with you is to break the vicious cycle. I will never doubt that it is hard to break a habit we might think is good for us, but it is only a cycle of mass destruction. Darkness wants to hurt us through such hopeless adversity, but it remains crucial that we do not let it write our future. We never have to let a vicious cycle keep us suffering in a sea of despair.

If there is a more significant lesson that I carried with me to the finish line with depression, it is that there is always a brighter light out there waiting for every single person. We may not see it all the time, but it is there in the deepest corner we never thought existed. I can testify to that through my own dark, traumatic experiences. The song "Whispers in the Dark" by Skillet talks about that light in the darkness and how that light handed down by God is always there, even when we become blind to it. I encourage you with all my heart to consider the song's message. Let it be a great reminder that there is always a light in whatever darkness life puts you through, but you must be willing to accept that light.

During the height of my traumatic battle, I thought there was no end to standing tall in sight. I let my demons take over while going down a vicious cycle before it almost became too late. I became so convinced that the darkness was trying to show me an empty void until I reached for help. The moment I finally turned away from the dark side and let help in, I realized the darkness was showing me the light in my story.

The hurt brought on by my trauma taught me lessons about life that the top of the mountain would never have. When I had fallen to the ground and nearly lost all sense of hope, traits still instilled in me today had been born. Trauma took away my childhood and most of my adolescent years, but it gave me knowledge and lessons I never thought existed. As ironic as it may sound, I do not regret going through the trauma I experienced as a child and teenager, even despite it potentially changing the course of my life.

One final takeaway from my journey is enjoying and living life to the fullest. Life is so much more than what has defined and made you out to be. I will never be the only one to say that your story reflects not what you have accomplished in life but how you have overcome those toughest challenges and reached your triumph. Always know that whatever challenges come your way are not meant to harm you but to help guide you. Always remember to reflect not only on purpose through the adversity you face but also on how you created your profound destiny.

Despite the negative in the world and life, miracles happen every second. Miracles should remain a sign that hope exists in the deepest, darkest shadows, so please keep that in mind. Every time I revert to my negative experiences, I remember all the miracles handed to me by the man in the sky. The biggest miracle of them all is my existence today. Given the adversity put into my own life, there is no doubt that I could have easily died a time ago, but I did not perish.

This is not speaking out of my personal feelings, but statistically speaking from the fatal potential outcome from my own experiences. So, I know from my bad experiences in life that miracles exist. Miracles happen all over the world every single day, and the miracles made at hospitals all over the world are one example of that statement. We may not witness these miracles handed down by angels when we want to, but we believe they are where we least expect them.

As you finish reading this, I hope you look back at your trauma and think about what good did come out of it. Despair does never mean a means to an end but rather a door you have been blind to because of the trauma. As I found peace and whatever closure I could find in my healing, I hope with all my heart that you, too, have found your peace and closure. You are more than the broken soul left by your trauma and do not ever let anyone tell you differently. There is a plan and purpose for every person in this world. It just might not be visible to you at this very moment.

It may never seem like it, but not everyone is a negative light, and there are people out there who would rather listen to your story and see you alive than underneath the ground. Never forget that certain circumstances occasionally break the world; you do not have to be. You can choose to turn any dark adversity around because it is never too late, but you must decide for your own sake. I will not put on a straight face or sugarcoat it, saying that while it is not easy, the positive outcome of overcoming the barrier will be worth it. I lost my chance to be a completely normal kid at an early age at the hands of an unfortunate diagnosis, but that does not mean every newborn child will meet that same fate.

For anybody touched by my story one bit, think about all the many other inspirational stories that exist. As always, thank you for taking time out of your day to be a part of my extraordinary journey from the greatest despair imaginable to the ultimate profound light. You could be doing anything, but you chose to open this book and read my story. I will always be thankful for that decision. I have read many stories like mine before becoming inspired by them, and I hope the same goes for you.

# Gift of Life: Special Thanks

If there is an extraordinary aspect of my journey from rock bottom to the profound light, it will always be every individual who has helped me see the "daylight" at the end of the dark tunnel. No matter the circumstances, many have helped me get through the worst times, even putting their situation aside. There will always be an enormous army of lights between my family, fantastic friends (including many who have turned into a family), and others who have stepped unexpectedly into my life but became an instant blessing. While there is not enough time in the world to thank every individual, I cannot end without giving a quick shoutout to those lights that have meant the world to me and those who helped make this project possible.

First (and foremost), I would love to extend a significant gratitude to the entire staff (past and present) at St. Jude Children's Research Hospital for all their continuous, challenging work in the fight against cancer. I knew from the first day I arrived at the hospital that I was in the arms of angels, and I was in a place that would forever change both my and my family's lives. Every single day, the hospital not only saves countless cancer patients but provides a unique symbol of hope to the entire world, a symbol stating that one day, cancer will be a memory. If you want a simple piece of advice on making a significant impact, look at the goal the hospital founder set out to achieve and how it became so much more than he imagined.

I certainly would not have made it into remission without the additional help of numerous individuals outside the hospital. No one asked my best friend Trenton to step in and do the unbelievable he did to help bring me home. He sought the opportunity to make a small but significant impact. I know both of us having the same caring heart passed down by our parents has always made our friendship as great as it has become.

I also would not have reached the finish line without the simple gesture of a man (my bone marrow donor) with the heart of an angel. The preparation period for my bone marrow transplant could have taken so much longer, even to the point of my early demise later in life, but thanks to fate and your willingness to help just one random stranger, you changed my life forever. As I have told you a thousand times, I will always hold your unique gift tight.

To my parents, thank you for everything you have done for me and for everything you continue to do for me, even in my dark times when I attempt to push you away. I know the situation between you has not been the easiest following the divorce, but you have always put your differences aside to be there for me, and that is a gift for which I will always be grateful.

To my two sisters and brother, I know I was the most enormous pain growing up, but there is no one I would rather have by my side and look up to growing up. Even today, you all continue to be there for me and support my future endeavors, and I will remain blessed for it.

To all my friends I met through both BHC and WIU, thank you from the bottom of my heart for showing me that the entire world isn't evil, even after I became blind to the good for some time. There is a light in the darkness, and you just must be willing to reach for it.

I would not be where I am today without my college experience at BHC and WIU. College should always be more than simply a diploma; for me, college became more than that achievement. I went from feeling like I would go nowhere in life to realizing a unique perspective and seeing a unique path for my life in just four years.

Teachers are so much more than just instructors, and every writing teacher I have had in high school and college turned into more than a teacher. Every single one has helped me realize my potential and, over time, helped me become the best writer possible. I certainly give a massive amount of thanks to you all. I may not be the biggest fan of writing, but that did not stop any of you from laying the foundation I revert to today.

There are still so many who have also made my existence possible today. My gratitude will always go out to every single family member, friend, and, most importantly, every medical personnel who helped me get through the deepest and darkest times and into a new sense of pride and purpose. Your support along the way will never go unappreciated. To have a shining light passed down to you by any single person is a precious gift one should never take for granted.

Lastly and most importantly, I want to thank God and music. They both were there for me when my life felt empty, kept me afloat through the worst, and gave me much more purpose than I could have imagined. Best of all, they both continue to keep me going through the challenges of modern life that come my way.

# About the Author: Jacob Mundy (Longer Bio)

Jacob Michael Mundy is an inspiring author and a resilient cancer warrior who has conquered life's immense challenges, emerging victorious since being declared cancer-free in 2013. Currently residing in the Quad Cities, he uses his passion for the storytelling medium and skills learned to help bring extraordinary stories to the local community in his job at a television station. Armed with an associate in arts and a Bachelor of Arts, he translates his passion for storytelling into a compelling narrative of survival and triumph. Jacob finds joy in diverse interests outside his literary pursuits, from movie theaters and concerts to hiking outdoors, exploring amusement parks, listening to music, and playing the guitar. His love for storytelling extends beyond the pages of his memoir "Profound Light," making him a passionate advocate for trauma survivors and a testament to a life reclaimed from adversity.